T0328357

ROMANIAN RHAPSODY

An Overlooked Corner of Europe

By the same author :

NOVELS

L'ÉCORCE DES PIERRES, 1959, Grasset.
L'AUBE, 1962, Grasset.
LETTRE À DORA, 1969, Grasset.
LES ENFANTS DE GOGOL, 1971, Grasset.
PORPORINO OU LES MYSTÈRES DE NAPLES, 1974, Grasset et Le Livre de Poche.
L'ÉTOILE ROSE, 1978, Grassét et Le Livre de Poche.
UNE FLEUR DE JASMIN A L'OREILLE, 1980, Grasset.
SIGNOR GIOVANNI, 1981, Balland.
DAMS LA MAIN DL L'ANGE, 1982, Grasset et Le Livre de Poche.
L'AMOUR, 1986, Grasset et Le Livre de Poche.
LA GLOIRE DU PARIS, 1987, Grasset et Le Livre de Poche.
L'ÉCOLE DU SUD, 1991, Grasset et Le Livre de Poche.
PORFIRIO ET CONSTANCE, 1992, Grasset et Le Livre de Poche.
LE DERNIER DES MEDICIS 1994, Grasset et Le Livre de Poche.
TRIBUNAL D'HONNEUR, 1996, Grasset.

OPERA

LE RAPT DE PERSÉPHONE, 1987, Dominique Bedou. Musique d'André Bon, CD Cybelia 861.

TRAVEL

MÈRE MEDITERRANÉE, 1965, Grasset et Le Livre de Poche.
LES ÉVÉNEMENTS DE PALERME, 1966, Grasset.
AMSTERDAM, 1977, Le Seuil.
LES SICILIENS (en collaboration avec Ferdinando Scianna et Leonardo Sciascia), 1977, Denoël.
LE PROMENEUR AMOUREUX de Venise à Syracuse, 1980, Plon et Presses Pocket.
LE VOLCAN SOUS LA VILLE, promenades dans Naples, 1983, Plon.
LE BANQUET DES ANGES, l'Europe baroque de Rome à Prague (Photographs by Ferrante Ferranti), 1984, Plon.
LE RADEAU DE LA GORGONE, promenades en Sicile (Photographs by Ferrante Ferranti), 1988, Grasset et Le Livre de Poche.
SEVILLE (Photographs by Ferrante Ferranti), 1992, Stock.
L'OR DES TROPIQUES, promenades dans le Portugal et le Brésil baroques (Photographs by Ferrante Ferranti), 1993, Grasset.
SEPT VISAGES DU BUDAPEST (Photographs by Ferrante Ferranti), 1994, Corvina/IFH.
LA MAGIE BLANCHE THE DE SAINT-PÉTERSBOURG 1994, Gallimard Découvertes.
PRAGUE ET LA BOHÉME (Photographs by Ferrante Ferranti), 1995, Stock.
LA PERLE ET LE CROISSANT, L'Europe baroque de Naples à Saint-Pétersbourg (Photographs by Ferrante Ferranti), 1995, Plon «Terre humaine ».
SAINT -PÉTERSBOURG (Photographs by Ferrante Ferranti), 1996, Stock.
PALERME ET LA SICILE (Photographs by Ferrante Ferranti), 1998, Stock.

ESSAYS

LE ROMAN ITALIEN ET LA CRISE DE LA CONSCIENCE MODERNE, 1958, Grasset,
L'ÉCHEC DE PAVESE, 1967, Grasset.
IL MITO DELL'AMERICA, 1969, Edizioni Salvatore Sciascia (Rome).
L'ARBRE JUSQU'AUX RACINES, Psychanalyse et création, 1972, Grasset et Le Livre de Poche.
EISENSTEIN, L'Arbre jusqu'aux racines II, 1975, Grasset et Ramsay-Poche-Cinéma.
LA ROSE DES TUDORS, 1976, Julliard.
INTERVENTI SULLA LETTERATURA FRANCESE, 1982, Matteo (Trévise).
LE RAPT DE GANYMÈDE, 1989, Grasset et Le Livre de Poche.
AILES DE LUMIÈRE. (Photographs by Ferrante Ferranti), 1989, François Bourin.
LE MUSÉ IDÉAL DE STENDHAL (in collaboration with Ferrante Ferranti), 1995, Stock.
LE VOYAGE D'ITALIE, dictionnaire amoureux (Photographs by Ferrante Ferranti), 1998, Plon.
LE MUSÉE DE ZOLA (in collaboration with Ferrante Ferranti), 1997, Stock.

TRANSLATIONS

UNE ÉTRANGE JOIE DE VIVRE ET AUTRES POÈMES, by Sandro Penna, 1979, Fata Morgana.
L'IMPRESARIO DE SMYRNE, by Carlo Goldoni, 1985, Éditions de la Comédie-Française.
POÈMES DE JEUNESSE, by Pier Paolo Pasolini, 1995, Poésie/Gallimard.

DOMINIQUE FERNANDEZ

ROMANIAN RHAPSODY

AN OVERLOOKED CORNER OF EUROPE

Algora Publishing
New York

Algora Publishing, New York
© 2000 by Algora Publishing
All rights reserved. Published 2000.
Printed in the United States of America
ISBN: 1-892941-11-2
Editors@algora.com

Originally published as Rhapsodie roumaine © *Editions Grasset &*
Fasquelle, 1998.

Library of Congress Cataloging-in-Publication Data 00-009590

Fernandez, Dominique.
 [Rhapsodie roumaine. English]
 Romanian Rhapsody : An Overlooked Corner of Europe / by Domi-
nique Fernandez; photographer, Ferrante Ferranti.
 p. cm.
  ISBN 1-892941-11-2 (pbk.)

 1. Romania—Description and travel. 2. Fernandez, Dominique—
Journeys—Romania. I. Ferranti, Ferrante. II. Title.
DR210.F4713 2000
949.8—dc21
                    00-009590

This book features many photographs by Ferrante Ferranti,
as indicated by the designation (F.F); others were generously contributed by the
Romanian Cultural Affairs Ministry.

Algora Publishing
wishes to express its appreciation
for the assistance given by
the Government of France
through the Ministry of Culture
in support of the preparation of this translation.

New York
www.algora.com

To Norbert Dodille
French Cultural Attaché in Bucharest

TABLE OF CONTENTS

Introduction

If the true history of modern Romania is ever written, it should be prefaced by these words: "Romania? seduced, ruined, and abandoned." Romania was seduced by the West in the 1960's and 1970's, ruined in the 1980's by the same West, and abandoned in the 1990's.

The story should mention the forgotten 1960's and 70's when the West opened its checkbooks to Romania, extending loans at favorable rates; opened its markets to Romanian goods, and provided technology transfers; gave her diplomatic prominence (Romania held the UN Security Council presidency in the 1960's, facilitated the Israeli-Egypt negotiations, and played a role in President Nixon's watershed visit to China); and gave her cultural and sports achievements top billing on the world stage.

This was followed by the ugly 1980's, when the West cut off Romania from credits (despite her being the world's only example of full debt repayment), cut her off from world markets, from energy imports, and from diplomatic recognition, and then sanctioned the political crime that was committed against her leader.

By the 1990's, international credits were frozen, the press turned negative (mostly feature stories on children's orphanages), and diplomatically Romania was reduced to a pariah status; her initiatives met with nothing but political demagoguery, absurd demands and invented crises.

Romania has always stood at a crossroads. Today, it is the only two-state nation in Europe, divided between the Russian military bases in Moldova's Transdniester region and Western-induced chaos in the rest of the country.

In this book Dominique Fernandez, a French traveler and writer, takes us along on his four visits to Romania (all after 1991). He finds himself confronted by a *post-disaster disaster*, and he is mostly unaware that Romania was in its heyday just a few decades before. In the late 1960's and early 1970's, Romania had achieved one of the world's fastest rates of industrialization, and life was good.

By the 1980's (at a great cost to her hard-pressed citizens, it is true), Romania had succeeded in transforming herself from a peasant nation into a producer of passenger-jets and a leader in nuclear energy engineering, while at the same remaining free of international debt.

*

Dominique Fernandez, unconcerned with the world of politics, searching for fresh impressions and animated by an unmistakably nonpartisan curiosity, is insightful and pertinent in describing the heart and the soul of an "overlooked corner of Europe." Perhaps it is time to bring dignity and recognition back to this European people, "the most abused" (in the author's words) of our times.

Claudiu A. Secara

Bucharest: The Museum of Art, formerly the Royal Palace

In Romania, as in Italy

Romania doesn't get good press. Vilified, slandered or worse yet, ignored, Romania seems to evoke little beyond scorn and disdain. This sorry reputation predates the communist regime.   Prince Antoine Bibesco, who was befriended by Proust during his years in Paris as a diplomatic attaché, would tell everyone that "the best thing about being a Romanian diplomat is that you can be sure you'll never be posted to Bucharest!"

Prince Gregory Brancoveanu, who fathered the poetess Anne de Noailles, had already relocated to Paris in the mid-19th century. Much of the high nobility along the Danube preferred life in Paris, especially after Napoleon III made a Hohenzollern prince of Romania. (Ion Bratianu, who later became the Romanian Prime Minister, had suggested offering the throne to a German when Moldavia and Wallachia were combined to form a new state in 1866.) Karl of Hohenzollern-Sigmaringen became King Carol I, when the two Danubian principalities were promoted to a kingdom.

The prestige of the French capital attracted artists (including the sculptor Constantin Brancusi and the painter Victor Brauner), and writers (Tristan Tzara, Panait Istrati), and the vicissitudes of the mid-20th century accelerated the exodus of figures including Eugene Ionesco and

Georges Enescu, Mircea Eliade and Emil Cioran. Romania's intelligent-sia not only chose Paris for their home but adopted French as their principal language. One would almost think (and many have jumped to this conclusion) that everything worthwhile in terms of thought and creativity has fled to the West, and that nothing remains in Romania but second-rate talent and hacks. And so, why would anyone go to Bu-charest, unless their job took them there?

So we assume that the Romanian capital has no cultural appeal, never mind what the political and economic circumstances have done to it. Even Claudio Magris, an Italian who generally appreciates Cen-tral European culture, calls Bucharest "the Paris of the Balkans," as if it were nothing more than a ponderous, primitive reproduction of the model of "the City of Light," the last in a procession of clumsy knock-offs, as you head east, and south, through Europe of the oft-emulated northern/western ideal.

It is hard to counter this opinion, especially after the events of the last twenty years, including the "so-called" revolution of 1989 (as many of my Romanian friends call it). All the recent news has destroyed the renown that Paul Morand had painstakingly succeeded in bestowing upon the city with his 1935 book *Bucharest*. "There's nothing left of Paul Morand's Bucharest," say the Romanians themselves, bitter and disillu-sioned. Nothing, I would add, except the fascination with France and the preference of French as a foreign language — even in the most Mos-cow-oriented years — and the remembrance of a writer like Paul Morand, who has been forgotten even by quite literate Frenchmen. The Romanians are fiercely ironical about their own country, and become skeptical anytime you try to say something nice about Romania or the capital. They are afraid of playing the dupe one more time, in this case over an instance of irremediable aversion covered by polite words. The West sold Romania to the Russians, at Yalta, and now they suspect that the interest shown by those who betrayed them and then ignored them for so long must only be a sign of malicious curiosity. Virgil Gheorghiu's successful work *La Vingt-Cinquième Heure* (1949), portraying the struggles of a Romanian peasant in Europe during the war, still ex-emplifies, for them, the equivocal commiseration that foreigners feel for them.

And it's true that no one talks about Romania except when some

Sucevița Monastery, built in 1585

scandal hits the headlines: the tragic fate of the orphans, friction with the Hungarian minority, a parade of striking miners converging on Bucharest. Romania never gets any attention except when things go wrong.

The media, which has created this negative image, never says a word about the beauty and the treasures of this country, its lyrical virgin countryside, the dramatic landscapes that flow from mountain to plain, from meadow to lakeside, to the beaches of the Black Sea and the marvels of the Danube delta, the charm of the towns and the splendor of the chateaux and monasteries. And the moral force of the people, their endurance, their courage and good heart, which fifty years of tyranny, obscurantism and misery have not brought down, where books are still prized as much as food and medicine, where you find more passion for matters that relate to the soul, more true culture, more intellectual curiosity than in the West where everything is easy and everything is commercial.

During all my visits, no one in Romania asked me about the scandals going on in France, from the schools to the immigrant neighborhoods. They can recite Apollinaire and Rimbaud by heart; and we don't even know the name of their greatest writer.

This book is written out of a desire to right a wrong, and is woven on a tapestry of surprise, sympathy and emotion. We won't be addressing politics, since I have no competence in that area, and it seems to me that the political life of Romania (reduced to its most desperate and bloody extremes) is the only aspect that anyone in the West might already remember, and it would only prolong the misconceptions and the poor esteem about this country if we reiterate its problems and harp on statistics that are unlikely to show it in a good light.

One of the most perverse results of the division of Europe into two blocs has been the notion that only the West is suitable for tourism, for pleasure travel, and that the East could only interest statesmen, political science buffs, and economists. Do we really have a right to be so ignorant about the physical reality, the qualities and the virtues of the people, the surroundings in which they live and the historical events that contribute to forging their mindset?

We visited Romania four times in six years, the same way we visited Italy and Spain while writing about them: certainly, determined not to gloss over any of the challenges that this people (one of the most ill-treated in the 20th century) are combating, but with the intention of strolling the boulevards, relaxing in the countryside, wandering about town and stopping along the way to chat with everyone, to take the pulse of the people. In every country the regime and the governing class are temporary, and it is rather the atmosphere that counts, the human resources, the natural beauty, the monuments, creations from the past and the present.

When we travel to Rome, do we think about who lives at the Quirinal or who is presiding over the Council of Ministers? No; so in the same way, on this tour of Romania, we will drop that discriminatory practice and ask, rather: what can we learn from this country, from this people, from their lives and their art?

HEADING EAST

In Germany, cars go 90 mph, in Austria 80, in Hungary they still manage 60; in Romania, they limp along at 40 mph. When you travel to Tanzania or China, after an interminable flight, it is normal to feel that you have been catapulted into another world: distant, exotic, underdeveloped. But it takes only a day to drive from Munich to Timisoara*, and it is surprising to be in an affluent country, all sparkling and new, a country of the 21st century, and to arrive the same day, after crossing three international borders but without any loss of continuity, in an antiquated country, worn, dilapidated, a country of the 19th century with, here and there, vestiges of the Middle Ages.

The progressive reduction of speed signals two things. You cannot drive faster in Romania because of the calamitous state of the roads, and the halting pace of the other vehicles. Rusty old Renault 12's (called Dacia's, here) with worn-out transmissions and worn-out retreads weave their way between bumps and potholes; never mind the carts drawn by horses, asses, oxen, and buffalo, often a whole parade of

---

* In Romanian, "Timişoara." When *s* has a cedilla (ş), it is pronounced "sh." *T* with a cedilla (ţ) gives the sound *ts* or *tz*: thus Tzara, the poet, is spelled "Ţara" in Romanian. Romanian names ending in *escu* (Enescu, Ionescu) are sometimes transcribed, according to a French tradition, as *esco*.

Moldoviţa Monastery: built 1532

Oradea: The Municipal Building and the Crisul Repede river.

them, and traveling at night without any light or even a reflector to let you know they are there; and flocks of cows, sheep, or geese that fill the entire width of the road; and solitary bovines or horses that suddenly decide to amble across your path.

Forty miles per hour, due to the deficiency of the infrastructure, poor maintenance and the habit (deep-rooted in the rural population) of regarding the road as part of the field or meadow; but also, perhaps, because of a wisdom that we have lost, we who are desperately rushing, who calculate in miles and minutes. What stupidity to curse against weather damage, obstructions, traffic jams! The slower Romanian pace grows on you: it allows you to look at the landscape, to pull over whenever you want, to take your time, to experience the journey. Everything is slow, savored, dense, everything carries emotional weight in this country. Even the word *Imediat* (with a sharp "T"), which is the answer to a wide range of questions. ("When will my order be ready? — *Imediat!*" "The road for Brashov? — Go straight, then on the left, *Imediat!*"). It is pronounced with a delicious slowness and fullness, as if trying to the impatient questioner the leisure to enjoy the irony of an adverb that is contrary to the national philosophy.

From Hungary, flat and monotonous, a vast plain where the wind of "progress" blew for a moment and swept away a half-century of misery, from Hungary that was modernized at top speed and is already reintegrated with the West, going on into Romania is like entering another universe and going back in time. Entering Satu Mare, Oradea and Nadlac, the first cities on this route, you cross the concrete border of poverty, lack of resources, outdatedness, and at the same time of charm and adventure. Gas stations are few and far between (and not always well-supplied); it's hard to find food and lodging, even in the cities. In what other country of Europe can you still walk around in the 19th century, presented with both the vexations and the promise of unanticipated joys?

At the Hotel Continental in Timisoara, a kind of *de luxe* hotel that tries to mimic the West, there are two elevators. But one was broken down, and the other went up only to the second floor of this sky-

Timişoara: Public Square

scraper. The rooms have no ceiling lights; in fact, the only light comes from two bedside lamps equipped with 25-watt bulbs. The custodians and the cleaning ladies spend the night curled up in the armchairs down the hall. This is already a caravanserai, a souk.

Timisoara, Romania's most advanced city, shines with a brightly lit town square, a new and beautiful opera, and an Italian ice cream vendor (selling at fabulously high prices, considering the local econ-omy). People here have a more developed political conscience; because of these advantages, this superiority, the city was the first to stand up, in 1989, against Ceausescu. However, as soon as you leave the town square, the *corso*, the opera, the ice cream stand, you find yourself lost in dark and deserted streets, and even Unirii Plaza, the architectural glory of the capital of the Banat region, remains deep in shadow. The old, broken paving stones are still in use, and the village green forms the centerpiece of the plaza, so that nothing would be less surprising than to see a flock of sheep grazing in front of beautiful façades with their high baroque pilasters, vestiges of the Austrian empire.

Romania's isolation, the sharp rift with Hungary (which shared the same destiny for so many years), the stagnation, the lack of resources and of fighting spirit, the inability to become modern, what are the reasons behind them? Two explanations come to mind at once. The communist regime, the nationalization of property, the atrophy of

individual drive, the pointlessness of exerting oneself in a system where there is nothing to be gained by working faster have generated indifference, neglect, abandonment, resignation to mediocrity.

Generated? Shouldn't we look for a cause that would predate Communism, that would be independent of the political environment? A feature of the national temperament? Something very old and very deep, something fundamental in Romanian nature? In other words, an innate tendency towards nonchalance, an attitude of *far niente* (or as little as possible)? Some cause that could perhaps be ascribed to the combined influence of the South and of the Orient? Where might these idle ways, this wisdom, this indifference to efficiency come from, if not from the indiscriminate mingling and complicity with the people of the 30th meridian line? The Romans, certainly, occupied Romania in days of yore and they gave it the name of Dacia. Many testimonies of this colonization remain, and above all the language, a type of new-Latin, rich in words that directly refer to the presence of the Roman legions. *Batrin,* "old man," derives from the Latin *veteranus,* a soldier who has completed his military training. Rome, however, hardly left an imprint of its virtues (order, discipline, rigor), at the shores of the Danube, or maybe only in the form of nostalgia and an aspiration to an impossible severity. Many other invaders: Mongols, Tatars, Slavic, Turks, erased

the traces of the first colonists. For several centuries, Asia contaminated the morals and the anarchistic vitality of the Balkan peninsula, reducing Trajan's Dacia to a bazaar.

Communism, far from introducing some rationality into this disorder, turned out to be nothing but the reign of privileges and emoluments, boyars and pashas. Instead of fighting the Eastern influence (as it claimed) with its centralized planning and leveling, it stimulated indolence and discouraged effort. So that these two causes: people's democracy and the proximity of Asia, combined to make Romania an advance outpost of the East.

Throughout this journey, we will ask the question: amid this general dilapidation, which traits are explained by communist management? Which traits owe more to the oriental influence? We will have an almost constant inclination to ascribe to Ceausescu and his ministers everything that displeases us — the ugliness of the city outskirts, the lugubrious half-light of the restaurants, the poor cuisine — and to the East, everything that pleases us —the lack of practical sense (or middle-class values), insouciance, lack of sharp-dealing in business, fatalism, humor and derision as revenge on the chronic failure. A Romanian proverb says, "How is the optimist different from the pessimist? — The pessimist says that nothing worse can happen. And the optimist says that, yes, it can!"

Our Romanian friends, however, would not agree. To say that what we like in them comes to them from southeast would be to wrong them as seriously as if we told a Milanese or a Florentine that the real Italy starts in Terracina, south of Rome, at the borders of the old kingdom of Naples. The Romanians reject their dealings with the Turks as the Italians disavow their connections with the Levantine and Moslem world, as the Spaniards repudiate their rooting in Islam. They want to be Europeans; they are horrified by their Ottoman past. In the last century, as their first prince and king they chose a Hohenzollern, precisely to draw up against the sleazy emanations of Asia the hard rampart of German virility.

Paul Labbé, who wrote a guide published in 1913 in France, already noted this aversion. "The Romanians are, and want to be, Latin, even those of the upper classes who would have reason to hearken back to Constantinople, Athens or Smyrna. But such origins are hardly acknowledged. It is axiomatic, in Bucharest, that Romania is not country of the Orient."

What could be more tempting, since 1989, than to blame the communist regime for everything that is going badly or not going at all? As if all this mess and impotence had no more remote origin. Asia, the Orient, is omnipresent in Romania. In both the negative and the positive, the good and the bad, the incompetence of the road menders and the talent of the violinists, the filth of the public spaces and the gold of the icons, the chaos of the economy and the effervescence of the arts, everyday and everywhere; not in a pure state, of course, but subtly mixed with the other elements, the Latin elements of Dacia, the German and Hungarian of Transylvania — an amalgam that gives this country its extraordinary seductive power as a crucible of complementary civilizations, the crossroads of races, experiences and adventures, the hearth of cultural cross-pollination.

It's clear, for example, that many of the monasteries and the churches display a mixed heritage from Byzantium, Cîteaux and the Italian Renaissance. And the folk traditions include an array of non-

European influences. In his memoirs, *Promises of the Equinox,* Mircea Eliade explains why, as a young scholar, he turned toward the religions of Asia. In publishing *Yoga,* the first of his studies on Hinduism, he felt infinitely closer to the spiritual universe of the Romanian peasant, and found it easier to render this universe comprehensible than to translate Kant as his university friends were doing. "The existence of common elements in the Indian, Mediterranean and Balkan popular cultures proved, in my eyes, that it was *here,* with us, that this instinctive feeling of universality existed which, far from being conceived in an abstract way, was the fruit of a long common history, that of rural civilizations. It was us, the Europeans of the East, who served as a bridge between the West and Asia."

Note the term "Balkan," which is so much harder to acknowledge, so much less glorious than "Indian." Eliade spent four years in Bengal and the Himalayas, not in Istanbul. The Far East, hovering in the magical distance, is considerably less frightening for a Romanian than the Middle East. It is not on banks of the Ganges that he fears to meet his brother in nonchalance and negligence, his velvet-eyed twin, but at the side of the Black Sea or, in Bucharest itself, in the teeming and parti-colored souks on *strada Lipscani.*

Ocna Şugatac: Mass

MARAMURESH

"*Mare*" means "Grand" (from the Latin, *magnus*). Coming into the country from the northwest, the first city one reaches is called Satu Mare. A little further on, Baia Mare offers an acceptable lodging, with the Hotel Mare, perched at the edge of so vast a plaza that no one bothered trying to cover it with stone or macadam; they settled for distributing a few concrete flagstones, here and there, in the immense vacant lot. The concrete buildings around the perimeter seem to be uninhabited, since there are so few lights. One bulb out of ten is working. The decor is solemn and modest: Mussolini on a tight budget. The hotel, to live up to its name, boasts a gigantic lobby, with colossal concrete pillars, a spiral staircase in the tinselly taste of American comedies, and clusters of lamps with the bulbs missing. When we arrive, one Saturday evening, a wedding procession is ascending the staircase, in the half-light, to the tune of Mendelssohn's *Wedding March*. After dinner, when my friend Norbert picks up his key from the large lady at the reception desk, she offers him a red carnation. She has noticed from his passport that tomorrow is his birthday.

Sunday, 7:00 in the morning. We are alone in the dimly-lit dining room. A sleepy lad approaches with his little notepad. In Romania, the various components of breakfast are ordered individually, including a portion of butter or jam, and are noted one by one, then added up for the total — a system that does not encourage celerity (or over-

Săpînța: interior of the church

consumption). The boy walks away and begins, with his dragging foot-steps, an absurd to-and-fro'ing, our first example of the Romanian peasants' extraordinary indifference to the Western notion of fast-food. We watched him come back from the kitchen with the cups, which he deposits before us, nicely arranged; then he sets out again; he comes back with the forks and spoons; sets out again; comes back with the paper napkins. Each movement, each gesture is marked by a sacerdotal slowness. Another trip for the granulated sugar, which he brings in a saucer. (They have no sugar bowls in Romania, and they have no mus-tard dish either; nor a salt or pepper shaker. The humble saucer is used as a universal container); another trip for the tea; another for the bread; another for butter and jam. Seven trips, when he could have brought everything on one tray. They do have trays in Romania. It's the con-cept of collecting seven actions into one that is lacking. Finally the cheese arrives, under the only two known species of this food product, *cascaval*, a pale yellow cooked cheese (*caciocavallo* in Italy) and *telemea* (a strong, salted white sheep's cheese), the salami and the eggs. Happy are those who ordered their eggs fried, or in an omelette. The boiled egg is perilous to consume, since the egg cup is as unknown in the countryside as the sugar bowl.

Beyond Baia Mare, over a mountain pass, lies Maramuresh. Mara-muresh! A name as beautiful and brilliant as the region that bears the name. We should write it in Romanian, once, with the cedilla that lends it such an exotic flavor: *Maramureş*. Nestled deep in valleys en-closed by the mountains, this is a preserve from the Middle Ages, a liv-ing museum of traditions. In Maramuresh the wooden villages are still intact. There are very few cars; quite a few tractors, towing cargos of hay or corn; and most of all, carts, drawn by horses (two horses usually, plus a foal trotting along at the side); with wooden wheels, sometimes replaced by wheels with tires. Splendid, pristine landscapes, without a sign or signpost. The ground is well cultivated, in small plots. Herds of cows, flocks of sheep (which feel quite at home in the middle of the road — and which the shepherd does not bother to shoo to the side). Some hens, but far fewer than the geese. Geese are everywhere in this part of Romania, squads, phalanxes, battalions of them. What do they do with all these geese? It is an enigma — geese are everywhere but in the restaurants and markets (and chicken is hard to find, too), and one is thus condemned to eat nothing but pork.

On Sundays, everyone dons the local costume, as naturally as we

Ocna Şugatac: Mass

put on a clean shirt. In this retrograde zone, the Middle Ages lasted until the 18th century. In Ocna Sugatac, the first village that we reach, the church (dedicated to the pious Paraskiva) dates from 1753. It is entirely built of wood, including the shingle roof, and it represents the type we will find everywhere in the Romanian countryside: a double roof above the naos (nave) and the pronaos (or narthex), a square tower girded with a covered gallery from which an eight-sided spire rises. The interior is divided into three spaces: the pronaos and the naos, square rooms decorated with blue carpets and fabrics hung from the walls, and then, invisible, separated by the iconostasis (here, made not of icons, which would be too costly, but of tapestries embroidered with flowers or faces of Christ), the sanctuary, where only the priest has the right to enter. These spaces are all of very modest dimensions due to the construction techniques employed. The beams are used only horizontally; they are held together by dovetail joints, without nails or screws. Iron was a too rare and expensive a material in this valley of cows, corn and apples. Tiny windows and, as the only ornamentation, a molding that twists about the main door frame and runs along the external walls, half-way up, like a frieze, so that the church seems to be wearing a belt. Is this an ingenuous talisman to protect such a frail building from the hazards of disintegration? The church has held up well: it seems neither young nor old, but from another time; robust, intact, cut from an eternal wood, a welcoming house rather than a holy place.

The young priest, in his gold chasuble, celebrates mass in front of several women kneeling on the ground. They wear headscarves and white blouses, with fleece-lined leggings tied with black laces. The orthodox service allows a certain freedom: people come and go, they move from the narthex to the nave, and nobody looks at you, nobody notices you. The priest himself, with the censer that he occasionally swings back and forth among the faithful, seems to be just walking around.

At 10:30, I notice some movement. Someone is carrying a table out, in front of the church, under the porch roof; it is covered with an altar cloth; the cantor carries his desk and his book outside; and the service continues, in the open air, for the peasants who start to flow in from the village and whom the church would be too small to hold.

Răstolița: the wooden church

Săpînţa: the "Merry Cemetery"

First, the old men arrive, and scatter in front of the façade, between the tombs of the cemetery. The men's costume consists of breeches of white fabric that stop at mid-calf, and a vest of black sheepskin. Some hold their straw hats in their hands, others, without any qualms, plant them on top of the gravestones. The women wear skirts with red and black horizontal bands, with colorful scarves and blouses. Men and women keep to their own places: the men opposite the church, the women on the two sides of the Circle; and they stand, in the middle of the lawn. This is gravity without stiffness, with the September sun beaming down.

The tombs are simple *tumulus herbus*. Apple trees wedge their way in between the crosses. Young people start showing up around 11:00. Two boys sit down in the shade. They use the arms of a cross to hang their tiny straw hats, which resemble an upside-down bowl whose foot is decorated with a many-colored ribbon. It's not clear how one keeps such head-gear in place; it's the badge, apparently, of rug-makers, tanners and weavers. The mass continues. Nothing could be more pure or more moving than this liturgy in the open air, associating the worship of the Lord with both death and sun-worship. During the reading of the Gospel, everyone kneels; the eldest, whose joints are stiff, just bend as low as they can. Knotty as the apple trees, one arm extended in front to keep their balance, in this twisted posture they resemble the charac-

ters of the medieval wooden pietàs.

It is impossible to describe, without betraying it, this scene of singular simplicity and nobility, made up of the natural beauty of the costumes and the gestures and absolutely free of ugliness. How long will it
take before industrial civilization catches up with this valley that, until
now, has kept itself apart from history? Five years? Ten years? The
costumes will probably disappear first. Television will impose the
standard model. But the practices? The feelings? The internal life?
The spiritual life? "What do you think of our spiritual life?" people
asked me. By "people," I mean journalists, intellectuals, people who did
not give a religious meaning to the expression. I did not dare tell them
that their outdated ways would make people laugh, in the West. And
undoubtedly these two boys, weavers, seated on a tomb, in long trou-
sers and felt jackets, are more self-conscious than their grandfathers in
white fabric breeches and sheepskin vests. But would they be happy to
have given up the antique purity of their rites for material advantages?

Sapintza, at the border of the Ukraine, is famous because of its cemetery. Every grave there has its own wooden stele, carved and painted in sharp colors, representing the person's trade (weaver, cook, mason, miner, veterinarian, butcher, shepherd, apple-picker), each one dressed in the traditional white breeches) or at the time of the accident that cost him his life (run over by a taxi, thrown from a train, murdered). There appear to have been several murders in this peaceful vil-

lage. On the stele, a small poem is engraved where death arises and summarizes the person's destiny. "I lived to a ripe old age, by making music." Music, apparently, keeps people alive longer than reading. "I read so much that disease carried me off at the age of thirty-two," deplores a woman leaning over her book. "I was wicked, and women liked me," — that's a member of the Securitate talking. The symbol of the communist party, which used to decorate his stele, has been replaced by two doves. A young woman protests that she is not as guilty as public opinion claims. And even sharper humor can be found in certain inscriptions where the dead is glorified for his faults.

Who is the creator of these impertinently naive ex-votos? Ion Patras, sculptor, painter and poet, died at the age of 69 in 1977. Pop Mitica, his disciple, has succeeded him. On the funerary stele of his master, he carved a small stele and Ion Patras at work, carving it. The art is quite alive. Several of these tombs are recent. In the village, a young man takes us along to see the house of Patras and the contiguous hut where Pop, who is out today, has set up his workshop. The paint itself comes from France, as can be seen by the empty pots left in the courtyard. We see old steles, in faded colors, their reliefs worn down, posed against the wall. "When a stele is too damaged, it is removed and brought here. Mitica makes a new copy, which is then replaced on the tomb." "And the original model?" we ask. "We throw them out." Ion Patras lined the façade of his beautiful house with wooden panels representing famous Romanian statesmen: Bogdan, Stephen the Great, Michael the Brave and others. In the middle of this portrait gallery, a circular medallion stands empty. "That was Ceausescu: he was taken down, and burned," the young man told us with an air of satisfaction that tells you where the revenge of the lackey takes shape.

As we are leaving Sapintza, we see embroidered blouses, bright red carpets, and lambswool blankets hanging on the balustrade of a wooden house. We buy a beautiful, thick white blanket from a rough and severe old country-woman, who does not want to budge by one *leu* on a price that is rather high. I like to think that boys with those odd straw hats, too small for their craniums, wove this ovine splendor.

The most beautiful villages of Maramuresh border the valley of Iza, from Sighet to Sacel. Rozavlea, with its church built of fir (1717), Bogdan Voda (1718), and Dragomireshti, whose church (1722) was transported to the Museum of the Village in Bucharest. The oldest of these wooden churches (1364) can be visited across the river from Ieud, on a hillside in the middle of a cemetery. Churches from the 18th century are not much different from the 14th century churches. For 350 years, the model was passed on: the same roofs, the same square tower with its watch post, the same spire with eight angles, the same interior distribution in three rooms, the same technique of wood-joining. The only change is that the twisted molding is missing at Ieud. This motif spread throughout Romania only since the 16th century, following the example of the episcopal church of Curtea de Argesh, the old capital of Walachia. In the Ieud cemetery, a big pig is nuzzling around between the tombs. At the top of the slope stands another wooden building, a kind of tower, short and squat. This is the bell-tower, set apart from the church and actually at some distance, since according to orthodox tradition the bells are rung only in exceptional circumstances. We will have occasion to discover by what poetic and appealing means the faithful are called to service.

In the parts of Romania where princes exerted their power, stone architecture was developed: Bukovina, Walachia, Oltenia. The exclusive use of wood in Maramuresh proves the persistence, over the centuries, of a civilization of peasants. The wooden church and bell-tower were the expression of the village, of the land. The word *tara*, which comes from the Latin *terra*, means *land*, whereas in the other Romance languages, the word for "country" (*pays, paese* or *país*) are derived from *pagus*, "village." Before the village, in Romania, there was the land, a territorial measure and political unit. In the middle of the countryside strange buildings, here and there, stand out: a wooden cross stands between two beams planted at an angle, all covered by a small shingled roof and decorated with painted or carved figures. This is a *troitsa*, a rudimentary shrine, a church of the fields, for the devotions of the isolated passerby. The tree trunk placed at an angle, pivoting on a fork and signaling the presence of a well, is no less holy. Earth, wood, water, and sheep, the peasant has no other wealth. He exalts them in plaintive and nostalgic tunes that he plays on the *taragot*, an instrument that may be of Hungarian origin — but may be far older; there is some evidence that it is derived from the Iranian *zurna*, used by the Ottoman janissaries during Ottoman invasions. The sound was so violent andso unbearable that the adversary fled without fighting. The modern *taragot*, related to the oboe, the saxophone and the bassoon has the opposite

virtue: it is impossible to resist the spell cast by its languorous and melancholic rhythms, sighing with the sorrow of the shepherd, the spleen of loneliness.

A Romanian village has neither main square nor a center: it consists of a row of houses on each side of the road, behind the double protection of a ditch and a fence. The ditch and the row of poles testify, perhaps, to the time when fortifications were necessary protection against the Turkish or Mongolian invaders. In the poorest villages, the fence is not made of vertical poles but of interwoven branches laid out horizontally. The houses are not close together; they are isolated in the middle of their own lots, and each one is beautiful on all four sides. To get through the fence and into the yard, you go under a monumental gateway, also built of wood, a tall construction with both a carriage door and a pedestrian door, under a shingle roof. Rich and meticulous details decorate the doors and the lintels, all lovingly carved. Among the most frequent motifs are the Tree of Life, the Sun, and the Snake, pre-Christian symbols of rural vitality and fruitfulness. In Maramuresh, where the art of woodcarving has been preserved intact throughout the centuries (some of these gates are new), a village street is a permanent sculpture exhibition, a window onto the rural genius. The church is neither at an intersection nor on a square: it is a house amidst the others, sometimes in the middle, sometimes at one end of the village, with its own ditch, its own palisade, and its gate like all the other houses, and its enclosure, not for domestic animals and agricultural tools, like the other houses, but for the tombs of the cemetery (and an occasional pig, too).

Bogdan Voda, the largest of these villages, has several rows of houses. Walking along the lane between the palisades, we peered in through one of the gates and saw a foal. The woman, standing at the threshold of her house, invites us into the yard. Her boy, Giorgy, ten years old, with a sweet little face under his woolen cap, is holding a book, *The Last of the Mohicans*, in Romanian translation. The mother wants to make a gift to us of milk, eggs, food products that cannot be found in the city stores (milk, for lack of refrigerated transport, eggs, due to a mystery of the distribution system). She would give us everything that she has. Finally, we are forced to accept a bag of apples: exquisite, these apples, small, wrinkled, and tart, the true fruits of the tree, not adulterated, not genetically modified.

Liliana, a friend from Cluj, then takes us along to visit a family with whom she is slightly acquainted. The Marish family lives in a brick house, the father being a mason. He is out, today. On our surprise visit, we find the mother and her two daughters, beautiful, fair-complected, with round and softly modeled faces, wearing their traditional costumes (like all the women of the village) this Sunday: wide skirts over petticoats, long, shoes with a heel, embroidered blouses, and embroidered jackets that do not close in front. They absolutely insist on keeping us to lunch. While one lights a fire in the stove, the others pour into a large cauldron all the provisions of the house: cornmeal, water, salt, lard, cream, and cheese, which they mix using a wooden paddle. While the mix is simmering, they take us for a tour of the rooms, and tell us about the carpet and the wall-hangings. There's not much furniture, apart from the high beds with embroidered covers. Then we sit down near the stove and have our first taste of the mixture, the delicious *mamaliga*, which is the national dish and makes up a meal in itself, a kind of enriched polenta, real comfort food, that one speeds along its way with a shot of *tsuica*, the virile plum brandy.

Near to the old wooden church, a stone church is under construction. From the looks of it, it is going to be large and jarring, both in terms of size and materials. The first offensive of ugliness, in the phase before the Coke ads appear. Radu Ionesco, a member of the Commission on Historic Buildings, in Bucharest, would explain to me that "The priests would like to get rid of the wooden churches and replace them with new buildings. We have the greatest difficulty in preventing them." Among the rumors that were circulated in France, one suggested that Ceausescu had razed the old villages to cut down the churches. That is true only in Moldova, in the grain-bearing lands, and the motivation was not pure vandalism but to increase the amount of land under cultivation. There is more to fear, for the Romanian patrimony, from certain priestly initiatives. They supported Ceausescu at one time, and then they supported Iliescu, the "reformed Communist" candidate (September 1992). There's no getting away from it — these remote country villages where time stands still, these pure landscapes with their beauty intact, these hospitable populations are the places where Iliescu's score was the best. In Maramuresh and in Moldova, the land of sublime monasteries. In a country of priests, pigs, apples, and carved wooden gates, how could the democratic consciousness develop given such surroundings?

I had promised to keep quiet about politics. It's impossible not to share, however, the charming manner in which it was displayed to us, that Sunday afternoon, on the road that goes by Iza. A crowd suddenly gathered. A small band of peasants in costume surrounding a rustic orchestra of two violins, two guitars and a drum. Carts all decked out with ribbons, horses with braids and plumes, boys in white outfits, riding the horses bareback. Is it a wedding? The oldest violonist, with the spotted face and jowls of an old South American *facendero*, let us know that they were preparing to welcome Emil Constantinescu, the opposition candidate, on his way to Sighet for a meeting. A pastoral serenade for the professor with a goatee, spokesman of the students and the intellectuals, the hope of Romania. Even in Maramuresh, we saw his photography everywhere, on the electric power poles, on the fence posts, and on the uprights of the gates (between the suns and the snakes). One cannot say that his campaign was poorly conducted or that he failed to penetrate to the smallest hamlet. Nor that popular feeling was completely lacking, since this village lost in Transylvania harnessed the cavalry in his honor and engaged an orchestra to greet his electoral tour with sounds that Bartok would not have scorned. When will he be going by? Sometime in the next five minutes; or two hours. With regret, we had to set out again, without awaiting this historical meeting of country folklore and modern reason. A few miles further on, we did come across his procession: preceded by a police car and a half-dozen modest Dacias, which did not look to be in any better condition than the rest of the Romanian automobile inventory.

It is late, too late to try to find lodgings with Father Isidor Berbecar, priest of Botiza and a friend of Frederic. *The Blue Guide* of 1966, that I unearthed on a quay in Paris, refers to Borsha, a mountain "health resort" at the edge of Maramuresh and Bukovina, "a Tourist Complex" of two "well-equipped chalet-hotels." We tell ourselves that would be ideal for Norbert's birthday dinner. But Norbert has the 1981 edition of *The Blue Guide*, apparently the last, as this work was suppressed for having been too kind to Ceausescu. In 1981, they were still talking about "the Borsha Tourist Complex," but, by a curious inversion of time, it was now said to be "in the process of development," and the two "chalet-hotels" had disappeared, with their equipment, buildings and goods. We decided to go and see, nevertheless. There stood two gigantic hotels built of concrete, with steep slanting roofs (that's the only resemblance they had to any chalet), sullen-looking from the outside, and frozen and lugubrious inside. There are carpets and upholstered armchairs in the rooms, which could be pleasant if it were not for the lack of lighting and the rundown condition of the sanitary facilities. When you arrive at a Romanian hotel, you should always ask whether there is hot water, and from when to when. In Borsha, it's only in the morning, from 7:00 to 9:00, according to the receptionist's forecasts. No bulb in the bedside lamps, and the mattresses are as thick as a wafer.

More sinister still is the restaurant: disproportionately vast, empty, and somber, a good illustration of the megalomania of the regime that did not have the means to fulfill its ideals. We were the only customers. All the tablecloths are so hideously stained that we hesitate to sit down. A girl, who seems a little ashamed, agrees to change one for us. She returns with a new tablecloth, which, instead of twenty fatty aureoles, has only about ten. A sad sigh from the girl. Norbert asks for red wine. Another sigh, of denial. The same goes for the *tsuica*, the pepper, for this and for that. "Polish vodka, yes, we might have some." And to eat? Only two first courses: tripe soup and breaded *cascaval*, and only one main dish, the invariable pork. Norbert goes for the *tchorba de burta*; he affirms that it is always excellent. This one, however, he spits out at the first mouthful. We hardly fared better. The breaded *cascaval* is the dish of choice, except when it is swimming in some kind of oil. Horror! the pork is breaded, too. The bread-crumb coating, inflated like a sponge, drips with old bacon grease. By chance, one of the rare articles not absent from the restaurant is the *ardei*, and the girl, very pleased, brings us three of them, quite fresh and bright; the *ardei*, the sweet pepper, whether red or green, providence of the Romanian countryside, miraculous vegetable, is considered healthy because of its pungent force that sets the mouth ablaze, purifies the stomach, and cleanses the entrails, dissolving like soda the rancid lipids of the "health" resorts. A tiny glass of Polish vodka, however, would really complete the cleansing process. We talk to the girl, who obligingly runs to get some; she is as quick to try to be of service as we are doomed to be unsatisfied.

"I'm so sorry," she says, coming back from the kitchen. "The *barman* has left for the night, and he's taken the key."

The *barman,* yes, she used that word, she believes that the employee dispensing drinks at her calamitous hotel deserves the name. It's a touching fantasy, a way of convincing herself that the magic of an American name borrowed from the movies could dissipate the communist misery.

The moon is blazing in a crystalline sky, superb and frozen. We are not halfway through September and the thermometer, which rose during the day to 75° has now fallen to 32°F. A tour bus is parked in front of the hotel. It comes from the neighboring Ukraine. The travelers, wrapped up in blankets, are planning to sleep inside the vehicle. Two or three private cars are huddled together in another corner of the parking lot. Their occupants, too, are preparing to spend the night in their cars. Russian license plates. Russians and Ukrainians go back and forth through Romania selling all sorts of things on the black market, pins, combs, toothpaste, odd pieces of hardware, tool parts, nails and screws, which they spread out on the hoods of their cars.

In the room, the duvet is as thin as the mattress. How good that we bought the blanket at Sapintza: ten pounds of good wool, and it won't be too much.

Perhaps the single most important event in the cultural history of Romania was the Roman occupation, although it lasted less than two centuries, from Trajan's conquest (106 AD) until the evacuation ordered by Aurelian (275 AD). A close second would be the move to side with Byzantine orthodoxy.

The country was christianized as early as the second century AD. Around the 10th century the Greek rite, imported by Slavicized Bulgarians, replaced the Latin rite, with incalculable consequences. As Louis Réau suggests (*Romanian Art*, Larousse, 1946), opting in favor of Byzantium cut Romania off from the Christian West. The inhabitants did not participate in the French Romanesque and Gothic movements, nor the Italian Renaissance — even the Russians felt its influence more, as the architects of Bologna, Milan, and Venice traveled to Moscow in the 15th century to build the Kremlin and the cathedrals of Moscow. Without the Germans, who introduced elements of Gothic architecture in Transylvania via their Saxon colonies, the aesthetic schism would have been as complete as the religious schism.

Byzantine art arrived late in Romania, not before the 14th century; and it held sway there well into the 17th. In Iaşi ("Yash"), the church of

Gura Humorului Monastery, built in 1530

the Three Hierarchs dates back to 1639, and the monastery of Golia, to 1650. The most beautiful churches go back to the 15th and 16th centuries and are clustered in northern Moldova, in the area named for its beech-wood forests, Bukovina. Byzantium's influence had the effect of limit-ing art to the Church (no non-religious forms were permitted), and of proscribing sculpture as being a too profane a means of expression.

Bukovina holds dozens of monasteries and churches, often painted with spectacular frescos. Here, for convenience, is a chrono-logical list of the most remarkable buildings. It underscores Romania's late adoption of both Russian art (which had emerged in the 11th cen-tury) and of Western art, which had left behind the Middle Ages since the 15th century. The impression of unreality which the traveler experi-ences upon delving into these hidden valleys and discovering these mysterious treasures is partly explained by the feeling of traveling out-side of time, in a corner of Europe forgotten by history.

> Radauti, 1430
> Putna, c. 1480
> Patrauti, 1487
> Voronets, 1488
> Neamt, 1497
> Humor, 1530
> Moldovitsa, 1532
> Sucevitsa, 1585
> Dragomirna, 1609

Paul Henry's monumental work (*Les Eglises de la Moldavie du Nord*, two volumes, Librairie Ernest Leroux, 1930) remains the most complete study of this extraordinary ensemble of monasteries, hard to find and hard to reach, for the most part isolated far out in the open countryside, in a spectacular hilly setting and protected from the Turks and the Mongols by walled enclosures. They were used as places of prayer, as places of work , and as holy sanctuaries where the princes were buried. The tomb of Stephen the Great lies in the monastery of Putna, which is one of oldest, but which has unfortunately been degraded by restora-tions.

Not far from the fortified enclosure, the oldest church in Moldova (14th century) was transported to Putna to keep it away from the Turks, who did not venture far into the forests. The planks are assemb-

Suceviţa Monastery: built in 1585 (F.F.)

led using dovetail or fishtail joints, without a single bit of iron or nails. On the roof stands a wrought iron cross, with a reversed crescent as its base. Much has been written about this feature, common to the entire region, and characteristic of many Romanian churches. Is it a symbol of the victory of the Cross over the Crescent? That is a widespread opinion, but it is indefensible — for the Turks, longtime suzerains of the country, would not have tolerated such an insulting emblem. Another theory is that the crescent is the reduced symbol of the serpent, representing paganism, as slain by St. George. Actually, the foot of the Byzantine cross usually bears a flower; at Mount Athos there are many examples of this decoration; thus the crescent moon of the Romanian churches would be only an ultimate stylization of these vegetable ornaments — with perhaps, all the same, a cryptic, even humorous, allusion to the superiority of the true faith.

The church at Patrauti set the layout that would be followed everywhere: a square nave, flanked by two side apses and extended in the east by a semicircular apse containing the sanctuary, protected from view by the iconostasis; above the nave rises a drum and cupola on pendentives; and before the nave, on the west side, is a square narthex. The cupola is broader at the base and narrows as it goes up. The contour of the doors and the windows is outlined by a stone rod.

At Neamt, ten years later, an innovation was added to this plan: between the narthex and the nave, the burial chamber was introduced. The deceased can continue to follow the divine service, but, death being regarded as a stain, they have to stay outside the sanctified space. The external walls are decorated with glazed bricks and polychrome discs, a practice that was widespread in Moldova before the appearance of frescos.

Wall painting began at the end of the 15ᵗʰ century and flourished during the 16ᵗʰ. Four more beautiful churches, illuminated by their incomparable frescoes, are Voronets, Humor, Moldovitsa and Sucevitsa. Each one is located in the enclosure of a monastery, stranded far off in the fields, so that one can actually go all around its perimeter. Given the modest dimensions of the building, the walls are painted not only inside but also outside, so that the faithful who come from the nearby villages take part in worship can read, as in a book, scenes from sacred history. The plan, being set by canonical rules, varies little from one monastery to another, except for the colors. Each church has its dominant tonality. The blue of Voronets, mixed with lapis lazuli, combines

Voroneţ Monastery: built in 1488

with the dark background of the fir trees to produce a particularly marvelous effect. With the exception of the northern façade, often damaged by exposure, the decoration of the other walls is almost intact and
has preserved a miraculous freshness.

Interior paintings. Christ Pantokrator in the cupola, a tall, severe
figure. In the nave, scenes from the Passion. The Last Supper is presented in very tender terms: Christ gives his hand to John, who seizes
it in an affectionate grasp. Peter's renunciation is given an important
place because of the human value of this episode. Voronets is sober,
more mystical. There, Christ is shown climbing a ladder to mount the
cross. There is more movement and feeling at Humor and Moldovitsa.
In Moldovitsa, the votive fresco, which shows Peter Rares, his wife
Helen and her children, testifies to an already realistic art of portrai-
ture. Peter is shown to be Moldovan in type, while Helen is Slavic. As
for the Virgin, she looks like a Romanian peasant girl.

While the nave is reserved for the celestial Church and majesti-
cally displays the episodes of the life of the Lord, the narthex (preceded
sometimes by an exonarthex) celebrates the militant Church, and offers
the spectacle of the terrestrial suffering of the saints and martyrs, very
lively and picturesque. There is a calendar of the saints at Voronets and
a complete menology or month-by-month register of the saints at
Moldovitsa. The characters show no individual differentiation but are
recognizable by their fates (decapitated, drowned, shot with arrows,
burned, stoned, quartered, crucified), or by their costumes or their social conditions. The prophets are barefooted (a privilege reserved to
them alone) and wear long clothing. A beard and coat decorated with a
grid pattern for the bishops; long white robes for the deacons, who are
beardless; a beard, mantel and, as for the bishops and the deacons,
shoes for the hermits. The ascetics are naked, with immense beards.
The stylites, bearded and dressed in cloaks, disappear at mid-body into
a column. Shoes and long veils for women saints. Short garments,
boots, and hats for the torturers, but no beard.

Exterior paintings. Astonishing, and better-known than the interior. Voronets follows the standard program.

Apses: In the place of honor, since they are the walls of the sanctuary, the triumphant Church displays its glories, according to a meticulous hierarchy. Across the top runs a frieze of angels, in bust, each
holding a medallion of Christ. The second register belongs to the

Voroneţ Monastery: the church (F.F.)

seraphs. Below, the prophets surround the throne of the Virgin; then comes Christ, in the eucharistic form of the Child in the Manger, between two angels and two troops of apostles. Bishops and hermits occupy the next to last register, the last being reserved to the martyrs. St. George, patron saint of Voronets, is in the center.

In Moldovitsa, the martyrs are above the monks and the hermits, and Christ is illustrated by a lamb holding up the standard of the Resurrection. St. George is replaced by the Child in the Manger, in Moldovitsa, and in Sucevitsa, by St. John the Baptist. This divergence of details changes nothing in the general symbolism. These rows of figures go around the three apses. Paul Henry notes that the monks, at the bottom, serve as a connection between the earth and the sky. They attest by their presence that fidelity in the fulfillment of one's religious duties is the way to attain paradise.

The hierarchy is not only vertical but also horizontal. For example, the 54 most important prophets are closest to the Virgin, by order of importance: Aaron, then David on his left, Melchizedek, then Moses, on her right-hand side. Melchizedek has precedence over Moses: his offering to Abraham earns him this honor. Among the 60 apostles, Peter and then Matthew are shown at the left of Christ, Paul then John to his right. After Matthew come Mark, Andrew, James, Philip, etc., and after John one may recognize Luke, Simon, Bartholomew, Thomas, etc. The same rigorous order holds true for the 61 bishops and 65 martyrs.

Façades. Three themes are repeated, from one monastery to another: the Lineage of Jesse, the Acathist Hymn, and the Last Judgment. Almost everywhere, these are joined by the life of a saint and, sometimes, three secondary motifs: the Siege of Constantinople, the Customs, and the Spiritual Scale.

The Lineage of Jesse in Voronets is the best-preserved. A first vertical axis symbolizes the line of Christ's ancestors, summarized by the figures of Jesse, David, Solomon, Roboam, Josias, Manassiah, Jechonias and the Virgin. But, as in the West during the Middle Ages, the theme became complicated with other considerations. On both sides of the main trunk, the prophets assemble as an honor guard. No fewer than 130 figures, belonging to the Twelve Tribes, make this an immense emblem unifying the two Testaments. The Old Law in its entirety is convened to consecrate the teaching of Jesus. And that is not all, for, in a

Voroneţ Monastery: The Last Judgment (F.F.)

characteristic common to all the Trees of Jesse in the Middle East, the pagan philosophers also lend their support to the biblical prophets. Thucydides, Socrates, Plato, Aristotle, Pythagoras, the Sibyl, Homer, each indicated by name, collaborate in the apotheosis of Christ.

The *Acathist Hymn* is painted in honor of the Virgin. Its name indicates that the faithful would sing to it, standing up. It usually occupies the southern wall, except in Voronets where, placed on the northern wall, it has suffered severe deterioration. The hymn is sung in 24 stanzas, the first twelve illustrating the life of the Virgin, the others reporting the symbolic episodes (the protective Virgin, the Virgin dazzling the faithful with her brilliance, the Virgin in a circle of rhetoreticians, etc.). The Burning Bush is sometimes a corollary of this image; it symbolizes Mary's virginity, in the form of a rock crowned with a large bunch of flowers from which the Virgin and the Child emerge in a medallion. Moses is illustrated in a posture of adoration.

The Siege of Constantinople. This is another corollary of the Acathist Hymn, but it is depicted only twice, in Humor and Moldovitsa. This is not a reference to the 1453 siege, which ended in the victory of the Turks and the weakening of Christendom, but that of 626 AD, where the Persians were repulsed thanks to the intercession of the Virgin. The fresco depicts a fortress attacked by sea and by land and, inside the walls, a procession carrying a banner with the image of Christ. The two sieges were fused in the imagination of the painters: the besiegers are Turks, wearing turbans and, an obvious anachronism, carrying guns.

The Last Judgment occupies the western wall, above the entrance, to remind the faithful that Christian life leads to one point in time. In Voronets, the entrances are at the north and the south, but still this painting is placed on the western wall.

It has five registers, from top to bottom. At the top, the Ancient One is in the center of Heaven, whose gates are open. Two angels are folding up a scroll bearing the signs of the zodiac, according to the verse of the Apocalypse: "And the sky was withdrawn like a rolled parchment," indicating that the end of time had come. In the next register Christ, his feet resting on winged wheels of fire, stands between the twelve Apostles, who are detached to the celestial militia in a profusion of gilded haloes. The third register shows the empty Throne that

Sucevița Monastery: the celestial spiritual ranking (F.F.)

awaits the Judge, between (on one side) the Elect, divided between prophets, bishops, martyrs, and hermits and, on the other side, those chose not to believe and who will therefore be cast into eternal darkness. Next we see the weighing of the hearts, a scene that allows for comic confrontations between angels and demons. Lastly, a luminous garden representing Paradise and, on the opposite side, the Resurrection showing the dead coming out of their tombs, and wild animals (octopus, whales, bears, lions, winged dragons, elephants) stretching and eager to take part in the supernatural event, opening their mouths and restoring the human remains that they had swallowed. The River of Fire that spouts out from Christ's feet carries off the damned to Gehenna, symbolized by a funnel.

Many delicious details deserve mention. The Elect are shown dressed for Judgment. They are weighed naked, to ensure anonymity and equity. They get dressed again, to enter Paradise. The rejected are not those who have infringed the moral law, as in the West — they are infidels, heretics, Jews in pointed caps, turbaned Turks, Moslems, Persians, Armenians. In Moldovitsa, catholic monks are included! In Hell, the damned remain naked.

Between the River of Fire and Paradise, the death of the Righteous and the death of the Sinner form a gracious counterpoint. Here, the angel strikes the deathblow with a lance, there, he collects the little soul escaping from the mouth, while David plays an instrument that represents not the harp but the Moldovan *cobza*, a kind of guitar. We often noticed that the Devil was systematically hammered, scratched, and destroyed by monks or peasants who, in superstition of animist magic, ascribed a malevolent power to the image. In Moldovitsa, a demon drags the first Jew by his beard. In Voronets, some of the demons are presented in a fantastical mode, with faces on their knees and bellies. At the very bottom of the fresco, Earth, in a pointed hat, helps along the Resurrection as best she can by raising the lids off the tombs, while the Sea, likewise personified as a goddess, returns a ship that she had previously swallowed up.

Complementary scenes. Sometimes the story of Genesis is painted on a space that was still blank, with an episode drawn from a popular legend, "Adam's contract." According to this belief, illustrated in Voronets, Humor and Sucevitsa, the Devil lets Adam plow his field only if he gives

Sucevița Monastery: the church (F.F.)

up his soul to him after his death: and that is supposed be the origin of the damnation.

The notion of Celestial Customs, or Stages, is illustrated at Voronets, Humor, Sucevitsa and Moldovitsa, showing the route taken by the soul when it sets out, relieved of its carnal package and escorted by its guardian angel. There are many obstacles: at each stage, it has to justify itself to the demons that stop it and display the list of its sins. It arrives in Paradise only after having crossed all the checkpoints.

One more topic turns up only in Sucevitsa: the Spiritual Ladder, from the first Judgment. The dead must climb the rungs, assisted by angels. Each of the thirty rungs bears the name of a virtue or a sin. I counted 52 angels, and 40 monks trying to climb. Fifteen of them manage to make it, and grasp the hand of Christ who awaits them at the top; nine miss a rung and fall into the abyss, the others are precipitated straight to Hell.

Lastly, several saints are honored with a fresco evoking their merits: Nicolas at Humor and Voronets, Joachim at Moldovitsa, Pacôme at Sucevitsa. In Voronets again, John the New, who was an honest merchant from Trebizond, is honored because the captain of the ship on which he was sailing, a perfidious catholic, denounced him to the exarch of Moldova as a Muslim. He was whipped and decapitated.

The two great figures alongside the main door at Voronets represent the Metropolitan Gregory and Daniel, the hermit, who advised Stephen the Great to found the monastery here.

A poetic alliance of theological models and popular superstitions, all these frescos vibrate and scintillate with color. While blue dominates at Voronets, green distinguishes Sucevitsa. The gold of the nimbi, the white and the green of the lower garments and the red and brown of the coats, the carmine of the River of Fire, the large white rectangle that brings together the Elect and makes reference to traditional Moldovan cloth, hemmed in blue — all these colors, so sharp and bright, create an infinite variety and make the walls teem with inexhaustible life.

Sucevitsa. These descriptions can only appear dry. How can we convey the surprise, the overwhelming emotion that comes over you when you look at these testimonies of an art that developed outside the flow of time? Every visit is an adventure. There are no signs by the road, no tourist apparatus around the monasteries, no snack bar or souvenir stand. Can you imagine Mont-Saint-Michel in a completely natu-ral state? For lack of protection, certain frescos have disappeared for-ever. At Arbore, for example, almost nothing is left. Elsewhere, resto-ration is underway.

Sucevitsa, the most imposing by size and the most recent (1585) of the painted monasteries, is the dearest in our hearts. We spent one night there, housed by the monks. Ceausescu by no means did away with the monastic life. In the narthex is a sign, imposed under the dic-tatorship, declaring this to be a "Complex of Romanian Medieval Art." Today, the monks have covered these words and replaced them by "Monastery." They would have liked to give us a fine dinner, too, if they hadn't been too busy preparing to receive a "delegation" the next day. The beds that they provided us were indeed the best of all our travels in Romania: tall, with thick mattresses and dazzlingly white sheets of a princely smoothness, with thick and fluffy duvets. As for the breakfast,

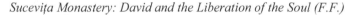

Sucevița Monastery: David and the Liberation of the Soul (F.F.)

we've never had such quality, before or since. They treated us, in their refectory, to fresh milk from their cows, eggs from their hens, jam from the fruits of their garden, all fresher and more flavorful than anything you can find in a store. Meanwhile, they were preparing the table for a feast. The Romanian Minister for Telecommunications had just arrived, with his German counterpart. An embroidered white tablecloth, a vase of carnations, four glasses at each place setting. We saw the procession arriving at midday, accompanied by four women from the village in costume (fur trim at the cuffs, embroidered blouses), who would greet the visitors at the gate with the triple ritual offering of salt, bread, and wine. This was tradition's homage to modernity. In the antiquated land where these souls grew up apart from modern development, wireless communication technologies must be as extraordinary and unsettling as seeing the deceased flitting by.

You would not suspect the sad history of the monastery from the solitude that surrounds it, the peaceful little valley where it is snuggled, at the foot of a pleasant wooded hill. The founders died in exile or were poisoned. Elisabeth, the wife of Prince Simeon, one of the assassinated founders, was taken captive by the Turks in 1616. In despair, she cut off her two chestnut braids and sent them to the monastery, in a silver box that one may still see today, suspended with a large candelabrum in the church, between some ostrich eggs. These vicissitudes explain why the painters avoided, in this case, the story of the Siege of Constantinople: this time the Virgin had not been able to defend the unfortunate princess from the Turks. Probably for the same reason, the niche of the sanctuary (usually reserved for an image of the Madonna) is occupied by the Ascension.

The interior frescos show a fresh sense of the landscape and of anecdote. Rocks, trees, sheep and the Burning Bush stand out with precision. Cities rise in high towers and pyramidal roofs. A Life of Moses, with forty scenes, fills the room of tombs; the altar of the prophet resembles a Moldovan church. In the narthex there is a complete menology, a whole crowd of figures including the Seven Councils, the Life of Saint George, and the Life of Saint Nicholas. A crowd of picturesque details attests to artistic "progress." Two restive mules, led by a whip-wielding driver, is bringing in the relics of Saint Stephen; another mule, struck on the head, sits back on its haunches, its mind

The Neamţ Fortress: Residence of Ştefan the Great (1457-1504)

made up not to take one more step for this brute. A fully-rigged caravelle is delivering the remains of St. John Chrysostom and sails for shore where a procession awaits.

Another innovation is a kind of cable, or roll, knotted here and there, that delimits the compartments. This ornament in unknown in the rest of Bukovina, and according to Paul Henry, must have come from a Wallachian model.

The exo-narthex is also covered with frescos, with a gigantic Last Judgment, and various symbolic scenes, the Wisdom of Solomon, the Song of Nebuchednezar, Gideon's Fleece, and different stories, the Lives of St. John the Baptist, Abraham, and John the New.

The external frescos display the usual topics, but on a remarkably large scale. Seven registers of figures cover the apses. Subtle geometrical drawings cover the bishops' robes. St. John the Baptist, with a pair of wings and dressed in a camel's hair tunic, is found in the lower register, with his lopped-off head in his arms, standing between the naked hermits whose beards reach the ground.

Jesse's family tree is more developed here than elsewhere. The painters, however, seem to have forgotten the meaning of what they were doing. The Greek philosophers, instead of framing the central tree, are arranged below it. Some bear incomprehensible names: Goliud, Umid, Vason, Selim (Solon?), Astakoe: products of imagination or deteriorations of poorly-recopied names?

Significant alternatives to the Siege of Constantinople crop up as the complementary scenes to the Acathist Hymn. The Crowning of Mary is a theme imported from the West: a late influence from Italian art, recognizable also in the 24-stanza of the Acathist Hymn, in the large cloak worn by the Virgin; she shelters the faithful under it, like a tent. As for the painting of the Pokrov, or the Feast of the Veil, it is a specifically Russian motif. The cathedral that forms the basis for the scene exhibits the five gilded cupolas found in Muscovite architecture.

But although Romanian painting seems to have opened up to foreign influences at the end of the 16th century, one also notes the renewal of certain local legends in Sucevitsa. The tribulations of Adam are described at length in the Genesis, including the famous Contract. Adam, in long red robe, unfurls a parchment before the Devil (who is yellow and naked, and deprived of sex). The glory of Sucevitsa remains the Spiritual Ladder, which occupies the entire height of the northern wall.

The ladder divides the scene diagonally: at the top, right, are the angels and the elect; at the bottom, left, are the damned. They slip off the rungs and tumble headfirst down the shaft, scolded by gray bats, demons dressed in loincloths and armed with pointed teeth, grimacing, with beards down to their bellies. A double-bodied monster with three enormous green heads appears at the mouths of Hell. The fight between good and evil, merciless and unceasing, that is how life was depicted in these landscapes that laugh all summer but are so hard during the long winter.

For dinner, we went to a nasty inn two or three miles down the road, where we found a fatty piece of pork — food that is far inferior to the succulent *sarmale*, tender cabbage leaves wrapped around rice and seasoned ground meat with sour cream and dill — that would be served to the Ministers the following day. The full moon shone hard in the pure sky, unmarred by surrounding street lights; and we walked back, this night of September 14, to the monastery. The watchman, who was expecting us, shut the gate behind us. The church suddenly appeared before us, set ablaze by the scintillating rays of a thousand spangles. The white of the haloes, the white of the mantles, the white cloaks with geometrical drawings, the white background of the scenes devoted to Adam (symbol of the light of God), all these light parts stood out with an exceptional force and a glare. All the characters, who showed a certain discretion during the day, took advantage of the darkness and silence to blaze upon us with their splendor.

The following day morning we were awakened by the singing of birds in the trees. We had hoped to hear the bells; but this was much more beautiful. The bells are rarely sounded in Romania. The bell-tower is generally set apart from the church and, in days of yore, no one went in except to sound an alarm when an invader was approaching. Nowadays, they are rung only at the time of some solemn festival. However, we saw a nun step out of the monastery. She was carrying a long, narrow board on her left shoulder, the *toaca*, and in her right hand she held a mallet. To call the people to worship, she made a turn around the church, striking the board with the mallet, sometimes in the center, sometimes toward the ends, producing higher and lower notes, and sounding out an actual tune. In front of the image of St. John the Baptist, painted in the middle apse on the external face of the sanctuary, she prostrated herself and made the sign of the cross three times, under the eye of the naked hermits dressed only in their beards.

One last surprise awaited us. In front of the gate of the monastery, a young man about fifteen years old was raking up the first dead leaves with a rudimentary brush. Under his astrakhan hat was an uncommonly sweet face — a Latin smoothness with Slavic mystery — and he inclined his head a little and smiled at us. After letting himself be photographed once or twice, he suddenly disappeared — either he feared, as some Romanian peasants do, that part of his being would be stolen with the image, or he was suddenly ashamed to have been caught at such a common occupation. Or was he an angel from the apse, descended from the second row, or a seraph from the higher plank, hiding under his rustic worker's coat his red wings trimmed with white? Or a demon, Lucifer after the fall. In Sucevitsa, as on the walls of any church in Bukovina, there is no sign of Purgatory. There is no middle ground: you either make it to Paradise, or wind up in Hell.

The latest of the great monasteries, Dragomirna, was not painted on the outside. The nave is unusually high and is disproportionate to the building, which nevertheless has a proud look as it stands in the middle of the fortified enclosure. There are seven steps between the narthex and the nave, representing the seven days of creation. The columns are divided into three rows, which are interlaced according to a geometrical plan, symbolizing the Holy Trinity and, at the same time, the meeting of the three principalities, Moldova, Wallachia and Transylvania, in 1602, under the leadership of Michael the Brave, seven years before the monastery was built. On the outside, the roll that girds the church horizontally, the ornamentation borrowed from Wallachian churches, is also made of three interlaced cords.

At nightfall, we listened as three young monks, close to the priest in his gold chasuble, stood in front of a swiveling lectern singing psalms and litanies. The deserted church was melting into the night; never have purer voices enlightened the darkness.

ŒDIPUS

After the monasteries, we headed to the farthest north of Bukovina, almost to the Ukrainian border, in search of George Enescu's family home. He grew up in the village of Liveni — hardly a village, more like a few dwellings scattered in a small valley. The composer's parents had a pristine white *izba*, relatively roomy, decorated on the front with a gallery and a porch with pillars. It looks out toward an immense horizon across a desolate plain. Even the sheep are black, accentuating the sadness of the landscape. From September on, the peasants wear their astrakhan hats. This part of Moldova justifies the pessimism of philosopher Mircea Eliade, who attributed his powerful tendency toward melancholy and depression to his Moldovan roots, and he claimed that only the hard vitality of his ancestors, horsebreeders in the plains of the Danube, helped him survive. Where did Enescu get his character, his energy, his capacity for work? From contact with the Gypsies, who supposedly were his initiators and his first Masters?

Such an assumption is revolting to Romanians. In a collection of essays published in 1985, a certain Mircea Voicana takes umbrage at the notion that itinerant violonists could have awakened the musical sense of this child of Moldova. Calumny! exclaim the historians. "Enescu's first musical impressions would have come from the *peasant* folk music

Bucharest: Cantacuzino Palace — "George Enescu" Museum

(his emphasis) and not from that of the fiddlers. And if we insist on asking who, besides his father and mother, might unconsciously have been the great Enescu's first 'instructor' in music, then here is the answer: the Romanian peasant, villagers of the modest Liveni." This is recognizable as an example of the official doctrines of the Communists, and their aesthetic nationalism that forbids imputing to a great man foreign influences, but also a visceral animosity, a racism that was cultivated by the Communists but preexisted their regime, the will to deny, against any probability, that the vagabond musicians might have had any role in the education of most famous of Romanian composers.

I suggest that he fell under the spell of the Gypsies, and as proof I suggest that he had to make an enormous effort to counter their influence. When he wanted to give his country a national opera, he wrote his *Œdipus* to a French libretto. As if, to protect himself from the influence of an ethnic group that so strikingly demonstrates its non-European roots, he felt obliged to ask Paris for a literary antidote.

Enescu's unique and splendid opera, where every sparkling facet, all the contradictions, all the richness of Romanian culture are reflected, this masterpiece was fully orchestrated only in 1931, and was created in 1936, in Paris, after a quarter-century of gestation. Enescu had chosen its subject in 1909, following a presentation of *Œdipus Rex* at the Comédie-Française. Sophocles' play, put on by Mounet-Sully, had stunned him. Œdipus, the myth wherein the ancient Greece of elementary instinct meets the classical Greece of intellectual control; the tragedy of the unequal combat between a desperate courage and an inexorable fate. A young Romanian could not have found a more beautiful opportunity to stage a representation of the collective drama of his fatherland, through the singular fate of one man.

At the age of twenty-eight, he had already had a rich musical life. When he was four, in 1885, his father made him his first violin; at five he was already studying music theory with a teacher from Iasi. From seven to thirteen, he studied in Vienna and, working directly with Brahms, was introduced to German classicism. From fourteen to eighteen years, he (together with Maurice Ravel and Florent Schmitt) studied composition in Paris, under the wand of Massenet, then of Fauré. At the age of twenty, he had already written many works including *Romanian Suites, A Romanian Poem,* and *Romanian Rhapsodies,* but also, distinct from any folklore, his first two sonatas for violin and piano, his

first sonata for violoncello and piano, his first quintet for piano and strings, and the octet. One can readily imagine, based on this brief life history, how he must have been torn between the heritage of his native soil and the need for opening the local tradition to "European influences." He launched a magnificent international career, but continued to come back to his own country on a regular basis, to Bucharest and even to Iasi (the capital of Moldova), playing the violin or the piano, conducting, and teaching. Two of the greatest musicians of the 20th century, Yehudi Menuhin and Dinu Lipatti, were his pupils in Paris and in Romania. He spent the war years in Romania, and left in 1946 for New York, then Paris, where he died in 1955.

Edmond Fleg, who wrote the libretto for *Œdipus* at the request of Enescu, was known as a poet and one of the best representatives of the culture of Israel (in the French language). So he was a Jew, who brought to his music the echoes of the wandering life of his people, such as Enescu would have recognized from the Gypsies of his childhood — but at the same time a poet of the French language, a delegate of the Western Verb. And what is *Œdipus*, if not a long and sympathetic exposé of the conflict between a relentless curse and a man's effort to thwart it? Fleg and Enescu designed their character as a model of will, clarity and energy, pitted against a perverse destiny. What Freud read into the legend does not interest them: no incestuous temptation troubles their hero, no "complex." Their opera remains on the high plane of the great Greek tragedies, they scorn to begin poking through the debris of the unconscious, to probe the mysteries of the psyche.

The topic of destiny resounds from the first notes, in the flute that plays a solo *doïna*, a melancholic musical form derived from Romanian folklore, a kind of liturgical chant, slow and resigned, but enlivened by unusual vocal flourishes. This *doïna* is reprised at the beginning of Act II, modulated on the Shepherd's pipes. Surrounded by his goats, sitting on a rock at the intersection of three roads, he is secondary character if we are to judge only by the limited number of measurements that he sings. However, the Shepherd represents an important symbol. Just as he ends his plaint on a despairing sob, Œdipus arrives along one of the roads, then Laïos by another. The son kills his father, right under the Shepherd's eyes, and he thus becomes the witness and reporter of the crime. You would need to have traversed the Romanian landscape and

Shepherd from Maramureş (F.F.)

spotted, here and there, the solitary figure of the shepherd, wrapped in his sheepskin, standing amidst his herd in the vast expanse of the fields, to understand how much Enescu's Shepherd (a national emblematic figure) goes beyond the pastoral convention of Greek myth. With his flute and his *doïna*, which could come from nowhere else, summarizes the nomadic and precarious condition of a people whose borders are uncertain and whose history is calamitous.

However, nothing would be more off-base than to regard this opera as an elegy to Romanian misfortune. Fleg's and Enescu's Œdipus is a born fighter; he refuses to give in to fate; he fights to defeat it with all his strength. When the Sphinx, threatening and already sure she's found a new prey, demands that he "Name anybody or anything that is greater than Destiny!," he answers: "Man! man! Man is more powerful than Destiny!," with so much confidence that the Sphinx, outdone, writhes with the pangs of death.

This humanistic proclamation is in no way vague or rhetorical. Enescu must be projecting his own spirit here. Wasn't he, the son of Moldovan peasants, miraculously ripped away from an obscure fate and promoted to an international celebrity, the living proof that faith in "man," in his creative resources, in his vital force, can move mountains? On the condition that he extract himself from the superstitions of the Orient, on the condition that he oppose the flute of Asia the tonalities of the West. The choice of a French libretto was part of this strategy of combat, of resistance. France, the (supposed) fatherland of Reason, provided Enescu with an antidote to the Danubian "charms," the *Logos* articulated in the language of Descartes and Voltaire as an antidote to the bewitching pan pipes. As much as the *doïna* exalts the power of the forces that work against man and the melancholy of subservience to destiny, so the poetry of Edmond Fleg (which is far more dated than the music) celebrates in its vigorous alexandrines the conviction that through reason, character and courage, one can overcome.

Who triumphs in Œdipus? To whom does Enescu grant the victory: destiny or human will? It is hard to say. In Act II, after the defeat of the Sphinx, the apparently-defeated destiny rises up again. Œdipus is brought to the queen's palace, acclaimed by the Thebans whom he has delivered from the monster. Suddenly, here he is face to face with Jocaste: and we hear the doleful tune of the Shepherd's *doïna*, signaling that the winner is only a winner for now, and that destiny will take its revenge by pushing the presumptuous one into the bed of his own mother. However, in the Act IV, the last, when the benevolent Eumenides welcome the hero on Athenian soil, he finds a kind of peace with them. "Was there a single moment, in my life as a victim, when I did not fight the gods who drove me?" he protests, before concluding: "Me, I am innocent, innocent, innocent! My crimes were never intentional! I triumphed over destiny! I triumphed over destiny!"

So, that must be the "message" of the opera: a renewed faith in human energy and tenacity. Nevertheless, what remains imprinted in the listener's memory, what has cast a spell whose magic persists over time, is not this willful creed but the melancholic flute of the Shepherd. Music's argument versus the argument of Reason: Edmond Fleg's experience would prompt us to have confidence in the powers of man's will, but George Enescu's music, the main force in this work, with modal inflections derived from Byzantine liturgy, the oriental perfumes with which each measure is infused, and finally, the stubborn return of the *doïna* suggest the defeat of the Western *Logos*, whose insistence still cannot drown out the tender and plaintive song of the wanderer.

MOLDOVA

Iaşi is not only the capital of Moldova: I felt the heartbeat of Romania there. Not that the city is beautiful. Like all the others, it has been disfigured. What accounts for its charm, then? Its peripheral position, almost at the frontier with the former USSR? A crossroads of Europe and the East, seedbed of great writers and original spirits, still rich in monuments and memories despite being rather dilapidated, Iaşi concentrates everything that I like in Romania. They say it was founded by a herdsman named Iashu. The cattle trade made the city prosper since the 15th century In 1565, reigning princes of Moldova made it their residence, and the city maintained this dominating role until 1862 when, after Moldova and Wallachia were united, the common capital was established in Bucharest.

During our first visit, we were hosted by professor Adrian K, a physicist. He has a beautiful collection of the French classics, in photocopies, since he was not able to get the books. This persistence of French culture, in spite of the geographical distance and the political vicissitudes, is one of the signs of the astonishing intellectual vitality of Iaşi.

The second time, Georges D., a Frenchman who founded and directs the five year old French Cultural Center, welcomed us in his es-

Trei Ierarchi Church, Iaşi: Brîul (The Sash) (F.F.)

tablishment; it's a stunning small baroque palace, opposite the University, renovated, painted white, and stuffed with books, cassettes, discs and videotapes, and furnished in a modern and cheerful fashion. Five hundred students come to take advantage of all kinds of activities; his extraordinary success fully justifies the creation of this outpost beyond the Carpathians. It should be said that Georges D. is a no common director. His Moldovan enthusiasm drives him to explore every road in the area. He advises us that only 40% of the roads are paved; therefore he often rides a horse or drives a 4x4 to travel through Moldova. He is so engaging that when he offers to show us some of his lucky finds, we change our plans and decide to come by Iaşi again when we return from Chishinau, in ex-Soviet Moldova.

The standard Moldovan dish is a copious portion of *mamaliga* (a kind of polenta) topped with an egg and mixed with tasty morsels of meat and sausages, topped with garlic vinaigrette. It is called *tokitura*. "Excellent," I say to Georges. "Yes, but if you had to eat it every day. . ." But that destiny does not in the least dim his ardor and enthusiasm. I have seldom met an official representative of France who was so curious about the country in which he was staying, who was so pleased to explore this *terra incognita*, this remote province where the daily life is hardly lacking in nuisances.

In Iaşi itself, there are at least three churches to visit, all from the 17th century. Historians classify them among the evidence of a "decline" of the Moldovan style. They say they represent the result of the natural evolution of the architectural forms that we first studied in Bukovina and, at the same time, an attempt at renewal.

The Church of Three Hierarchs, the oldest (1639), takes the form of a compact block surmounted by two bell-towers with pointed roofs. The exaggerated height of the walls, the heavy mass of the two square bases that support the bell-towers, are supposed to be signs of this "decline." One of the innovations would be the light abstract bas-reliefs that decorate the entirety of the external walls, with Syrian and Persian motifs interlaced, an extraordinary interplay of arabesques and lace — an indisputable influence of the Muslim East.

We should also note the *brâu*, which appeared for the first time in 1609 at Dragomirna, and which from then on became a hallmark of late Moldovan art, according to Paul Henry. This roll or molding, two-thirds of the way up the external walls, is imported from Wallachia.

The most famous example is the cable that girdles the episcopal church of Curtea de Argesh, northwest of Bucharest. There is also a cable in Dragomirna, twisted on only one side, as in Wallachia. At the Three Hierarchs, and in the rest of Moldova, the cord is alternatively twisted rightwards on the left and leftwards on the right. We have not found any explanation as to why the Moldovans went for this double alternative twisting; after all, there may be no other reason than the desire to be different from the Wallachs, from whom they had borrowed the idea. But why did they adopt the motif in the first place? Just out of a desire to try something new, to reinvigorate a style that was getting stale? Or was it a fetishistic gesture? Out of a conviction, for example, that the cord would magically contribute to the longevity, that it would help keep going, an architecture that was already considered to be on its last legs?

France, alas, was not always well-inspired in the choice of its missionaries. In the 1880's, the architect Leconte du Nouÿ, a student of Viollet-le-Duc, undertook a restoration at the Church of Three Hierarchs. The results were calamitous: the bell-tower, which marked the entry of the monastery, was destroyed; an outrageously overdone restoration of the interior paintings, with a profusion of gold and tinselly details. . . Almost nothing is left but the ostrich eggs, ensconced inside the great chandelier, to remind us through this symbol of the bond between the earth and the sky, that we are in a sanctuary, not a casino.

On a hill on the way out of town, the monastery of Cetatsuia is remarkably intact, from the enclosing wall and the bell-tower to the old Turkish baths, and even some monks. The church has two cupolas, and a *Brâu*, reproduced inside on pillars. The ensemble is powerfully suggestive, with a splendid view from the top of the rampart, looking out over the undulations of the countryside and the bell-towers of the city.

Lastly, in the heart of Iaşi, the monastery of Golia has also managed to retain its fortified enclosure, with a porch and massive watchtower with ogive arches. The many drums, cupolas and external pediments and, inside, the system of arches supporting the cupolas, indicate a Russian influence.

What no Romanian travel guide mentions is that in the 19th century, one of the priests of Golia was none other than the brilliant Ion Creanga, author of popular tales, a big, fat, colorful character, and friend of the eminent poet Mihaïl Eminesco (whom he entertained in his "shack," as he called the presbytery, when the future spokesman of

Cetăţuia Monastery (F.F.)

the Romanian nation was in misery.

Creanga was born in 1837, in a village in the eastern Carpathians. Every Romanian schoolchild reads his *Memories of Childhood*, with a selection of tales. The *History of Mr. Lazy* is not included in the school anthology, and for good reason. The story has it that a peasant, who absolutely refused to work, is condemned to death by his hard-working colleagues. A pious lady tries to save him, and gives him some biscuits for free. "Thank you very much, they are too hard!" he retorts, disgusted. He prefers to be hanged than to make the effort of chewing them. He is indeed hanged, to the great satisfaction of the village. I read this summary in the foreword to another book, where I also learned that Creanga got a lot of attention from the locals by using a rifle to shoot the clouds of crows that would mass in the trees of the courtyard that was in his sacred charge. I often noted the freedom of the orthodox service, despite of the gravity of the songs and the majesty of the liturgy; but still it's a surprise to find out that a priest could be the author of mischievous tales, and such was the case with Creanga.

I read his little tale from a photocopy that someone gave me, at the Trajan Hotel, which had very much improved in five years. Hot water around the clock, plenty of light bulbs, and bedside lamps. Ask for Room 101, which has a foyer and a salon furnished with a red velvet settee and armchairs — almost a baroque opulence. The bed occupies an alcove sheltered by red hangings. Room 103 is also a suite. The foyers hold refrigerators (which are empty), and you can plug them in and place your beer in there, which you can buy out in front of the hotel at an open air market; however, the refrigerators categorically refuse to function, in spite of a hellish din that shakes their rusted entrails.

The view from these two rooms, looking out over the plaza, is always animated and merry. Norbert points out to me a good-looking car, white, modern, some make that I do not recognize. Romania has set out to update its automobile park, to replace its decrepit Dacias. Renault offered a style that was obsolete in France. The South Koreans offered this Cielo, shiny and new. They won. For now, they export their cars; later on they are supposed to be assembled on location once the factories have been built. The Romanians wanted vehicles with a future, not obsolete models. They are eager to escape their chronic poverty and the gray misery of their infrastructure. The French did not understand this desire for revival, for rebirth after the long communist winter.

Iaşi: Culture Palace

Chishinau, Moldova

Across the valley of the River Prut begins the Republic of Moldova, which has split off from the former USSR. In Soviet times, the Russian name for it was Moldavia, and its capital Chishinau is the former Kishinev. The population in Moldova is 70% Romanian, 30% Russian. However, nobody seems to notice that this Republic dreams of being joined to Romania. The area — formerly Bessarabia — has often changed master. Alexander I annexed it to Russia in 1812. In 1920, it was assigned to Romania. Stalin occupied it in 1940 and the 1947 Treaty of Paris gave it up to the USSR. In 1989, when Moldova became an independent Republic, part of the Russian minority rebelled and, after a short civil war, proclaimed another republic to the east, with its capital at Tiraspol. In Chishinau itself, while asking our way, we frequently came across people who only spoke Russian. The two communities cohabit nevertheless without friction. While the Romanians are in the majority, the Russians have kept control of most political as well as economic matters. In the southern part of the country are Gagauzes, Turkish-speaking Moslems.

At the border between the two Moldovas, you can see the difference between the carefree Romanian style and the more orderly, more military organization. On the Russian side, the environment is much less personal, much less beautiful than on the Romanian side. The houses are all of a stereotyped model. There is an enormous number of motorcycles with sidecars. The outskirts and the peripheral neighborhoods of Chishinau are flourishing with small trade. A crowd presses around the displays in the open air; but there's not much choice and the goods are poor. This changes entirely once you make it to the center of town. Broad tree-lined avenues, pretty public gardens and well-maintained parks bring to mind a resort town; there are no boutiques or street vendors, just some large solemn buildings isolated in the greenery. These were the official residences of the Soviet dignitaries; they occupied this district exclusively. The palace of the Presidency has been taken over by the ministries now.

The colonial system persists. The Dacia Hotel, where we were put up, belonged to the Communist Party. It has remained in good condition — or so it seems. In Romania, when one arrives at a hotel, one starts by inquiring about the "schedule," i.e. the hours when hot water is available. In general, this would be two hours the evening and two hours the morning. In Chishinau, it's a superfluous question, even in the beautiful and modern Dacia: there is no water at all, neither hot nor cold, before evening. This shortage is astonishing in an area that clearly has sufficient water.

Moldova was considered to be one of the nicest regions of the USSR. It has a relatively moderate climate, plenty of fruit (we tasted excellent grapes), and decent quality wines. At present, the situation is catastrophic. There used to be an electronics industry; but they don't have any more customers after the collapse of the empire. The average wages have fallen to a fourth of the average in Romania. The minimum wages in 1998 were around $3.00. The buildings are poorly heated, or are not heated at all. The level of education is going down, the instructors are giving up teaching to devote themselves to business in order to support their families. It's impossible to get an apartment in the center: you have to live in the outskirts, where housing is assigned according to one's profession: teachers here, engineers there, etc..

Dan, a bright-faced young man, gives us this information in a soft voice. He is studying French, and speaks it beautifully; and English too, apparently, never mind Romanian and Russian. The director of the Alliance Française hired him to organize the courses. At $45 per month, he is paid twice as much as the average teacher, but with an eight-hour work day and ten times more work than any civil servant here. What would be Dan's future? He has no future, in spite of his four languages and many talents. The only way for him to make something of himself would be to get a job with a multinational firm.

Everywhere I heard the same story, the same resigned complaints — but I also noted the courage and the perseverance of the students. We met them at a meeting organized by the Writers' Union, a remnant survivor of the communist intellectual brigades. After a reception by the president and his staff, after the usual speeches (an unbearable display of chauvinistic rhetoric and doctrine, proof that the leaders are the same and that the Soviet habits of power haven't softened much), we were led to a room where a hundred young people and teachers were waiting to ask me some questions about literary life in France. They ask their questions rather freely, in spite of the presence on the stage, next to me, of the great (and great-bellied) president-apparatchik, who does not hide his dislike of being excluded from the dialogue.

Where is poetry headed? (Downhill, alas! That's the ritual answer to this no-less ritual question, in these countries where the poetic

culture remains alive and strong.) What themes are novels addressing? (An old concern of the communist regime, and not so stupid, when you get right down to it. I hardly dare tell them that far too many French novelists would be ashamed to acknowledge that they are dealing with any subject at all, these days.) Which school of philosophy do I follow? (Here, I tell them very clearly that in my country you don't have to join any system, that everyone is free to think whatever he wants. For this question is only a residue of the old ideological control; and my answer causes a certain astonishment in the room, and a more accentuated frown in my neighbor.) What is France going to do with its Arabs? (an allusion to the outbreaks of violence in certain cities with a large immigrant population; and I sense a certain suspicion against Moslems.)

A very young student — still a high school student, I was later told — raised his hand and said that he had written a French poem. From his colleagues' gestures, I gather that I must not restrain myself to vague congratulations but invite the young fellow to stand up and read his work. He recites several stanzas, in rhymed verse, where he combines various fantasies of being killed: sometimes decapitated, sometimes hanged, sometimes suffocated. The subject, the tone, the rhymes make me think of some Chatteron, a thin, consumptive hero from the 1830's, writing away in the obscurity of an unheated garret — and, after all, doesn't Moldova at this turn of a century lend itself to a blossoming of desperate romanticism? The audience does not seem to find anything out of the ordinary, neither in the youth's pessimism, nor in the public reading of such funereal confidences.

Calin is the young poet's name, a name that suits him well. After the assembly, he comes up to talk with me, with his parents who are both poets; with a Parnassian affection they protect their son, a thin and fragile flower.

Walking through the city with Dan and several of his friends, we discuss the Alliance Française. It was opened in November 1994, with five or six small rooms and a few books. While the physical equipment is modest, the people's enthusiasm is obvious. This gesture from France is highly appreciated. Of the Western nations, only the United States and Germany have opened embassies in Chishinau, so far. The French, who plan to open one presently, have started with this cultural outpost. The Moldovan cultural identity, Dan emphasizes, starts with Latin. The USSR Russianized the region in 1940. The Romanian language was transcribed into Cyrillic characters, Romanian books were

Moldoviţa Monastery: built in 1532

printed in Cyrillic characters, and the border with Romania was closed, putting an end to the national solidarity.

Paris remains the model for Moldovan intellectuals, according to Dan. But what do they know of contemporary French literature? He blushes and lowers his voice. "I know what you'll think. We only read Maurice Druon, the most famous, and two others are also studied here in class; they are our only references today: Paul Valiant-Couturier [he was editor of *Humanité* in 1928 and author of the 1929 *Let us defend the USSR* (against Panaït Istrati, probably)], and. . . Pierre Gamara." "Who?" I made him repeat the name. Dan, although he realizes that his country had become culturally impoverished under Soviet domination, is still shocked to learn that this pawn of the French communist press, here considered a literary great, is completely unknown in Paris.

In one of the parks, the busts of the great Moldovan writers are lined up under the shade trees along a beautiful alley. Except for one, a native of Bessarabia, all are Romanians from Moldova. They are the greatest celebrities of Romanian literature, starting with Mihaïl Eminesco, the national poet. I recognize Lucian Blaga, the poet and philosopher, and Ion Creanga, the facetious anticonformist storyteller and priest from Golia. "Did the Russians leave these busts in place?" They would not have dared to remove them, according to Dan.

What else is there to see in Chishinau? We had heard about an old Jewish neighborhood, a vestige of the ghetto where the pogrom of 1903 killed more than all the pogroms of 1881. Alexander III let popular anti-Semitism take its course every time the economic difficulties created dissatisfaction. To our surprise, none of the students who were with us knew of this district. We find it, finally: there's not much there, in fact, just a few dilapidated houses.

And how about the "blue church" that people in Iași had told us was the wonder of Chishinau? This time, we met with general and absolute ignorance. No one could even figure out what we were trying to say. However, this building, tracked down after a great deal of trouble, based on the always vague directions of people in the street, is the only church in the capital that is worthy of a detour. Pale blue walls, three bell-towers covered with blue cupolas, and numerous pinnacles with gilded cupolas; a splendid iconostasis inside. But all that, for Dan and his friends, distracted as they are with the dream of a vast and transnational Latin union, feels too Russian, too Slavic.

Ciurea: Mayor's Mansion

Dobrovaţi: the church (F.F.)

Ciurea, among the Gypsies

We get back to Iaşi, after a morning's drive. Georges takes us along at once to visit some of the places that he has discovered. Barely a few miles outside of the city is the village of Ciurea, a village of Hungarian Gypsies. Our first contact with the mysterious world of gypsies. I had ideas, many and contradictory, about them, but nothing that I could imagine resembled what we saw. The Gypsies of Romania have a representative in Parliament; he comes from Ciurea, whose inhabitants, scarcely settled from their nomadic ways, are still adapting to living in houses. Georges, sent as an observer during the last elections, made friends with the village chief and his family. Without this introduction, we never would have been received.

Did I call this a village? It is more like a random scattering of homes on the side of a hill, in the dust of unpaved roads. They are large, enormous, sumptuous, with balconies decorated with wood carving, capped with extravagant roofs of sheet metal. Pinnacles, towers, turrets, decorative openwork, and filigree gutters, this is a metalworking bonanza. Gypsies are tinsmiths by tradition, zinc workers, and ironmongers; and the covering of their houses attest to the creative imagination those Ciurea residents who continue to exercise their ancestral trade — just as the horses, that circulate freely in the alleys, recall the days when they were wandering.

The largest, most beautiful of these residences belongs to the village chief, the *boulibash*. Pagoda roofs, a luxury of balconies and galleries both open and windowed, so many that the ensemble takes on the appearance of one of those *Jain* temples that you see in India, overflowing with ornamentation. When it comes to color, the screaming bright paint in the interior cannot be beat anywhere in the world. Since the chief is on an errand in Bucharest, his son does us the honors: a robust young man, well-fed, dressed in an electric blue suit whose jacket with fold buttons comes up to his neck. He shows us around the various rooms: sitting rooms, nothing but sitting rooms, upstairs and downstairs throughout the palace! And all are furnished the same way, with sofas and relaxed armchairs upholstered in every color, the rawest and most aggressive possible. The earthenware (heating) stoves are shaped like big rocks. We see neither bathroom nor kitchen. The money and imagination seems to have all been spent in decorating every single room, walls and ceilings included, with hyperrealist frescos.

Not a square inch of wall or ceiling, not the least recess has not been painted, patterned with frantic meticulousness. Here, we see the son of the house, in the same electric blue suit, standing beside a little red car, an imitation Ferrari. There, a picture of reindeers under snow, or women bathing. Elsewhere, sirens are singing under a cascade. Peacocks wheel in the sky, wild boars gallop through a forest. In the back of a gondola, a woman flutters her fan. Red vermilion is a dominant hue, with royal purple, golden yellow, and emerald green. Everything

Iaşi: the Jewish Cemetery

has to shine and glow. If only one wall were painted, perhaps it would not look so good. However, when every surface is scintillating with multicolored images, it produces an effect of unquestionable art. To say "kitsch" or "comic strip" would hardly scratch the surface. The topics are worth studying, an imaginative, exuberant mix of memories of the old life, the adventurous life on the road, among the animals, and erotic fantasies ("the eternal female," eternally associated with watery landscapes).

While we admire the inventions of the painter (who came from Iași, they proudly inform us, but worked according to models of a "designer" from Bucharest), a small crowd follows us, and gets bigger as we pass from room to room. They are small and squat, with round faces. The women still wear the traditional costume, long dresses, shawls, in strident colors. Everyone runs to have a picture taken. Each of them poses, standing in front of a view of a lake or mountain. Nostalgia for life under the open sky? These murals probably help them tolerate the claustrophobia and the monotony that go hand in hand with increased wealth and upward mobility. As for the *boulibash*'s son, he wants his picture taken in front of his own portrait, beside the little red car. The image in the image. He places his hand between two buttons of his jacket, and takes up his position in front of the camera, semi-Mao, semi-Napoleon.

Then, the crowd accompanies us through the village. The house of the assistant *boulibash*, a little less opulent, has still great charm. The external walls are carved. You enter via a veranda filled with artificial flowers. Inside, striped fabrics are everywhere, and richly decorated hangings. A rose and yellow lamé fabric, brought from Turkey, covers the ceiling in rhombuses the ceilings. Jig-sawn lamps, shawls from Maramuresh pinned to the walls, in studied swirls. Some frescos too, the same universe of rivers, forests, châteaux; scenes of hunting and fishing. And, as a counterpoint to these evocations of a life of vagrancy and freedom now ended, here, lying on a sofa in the midst of cherubim, a half-naked *houri* with adorned with brilliant jewels.

We visit a few more houses, older, recently decorated by the same vivid imagination. The grandfathers of the young people who lead us around were still nomads. Decorative frescos, carpets, shawls over a table that is carved with a complex design, and patterned fabrics make each interior space an opening to fantasy for those who may suffer for the loss of independence and the charms and the emotions of traveling. A sixteen-year-old man takes us along to a house where he lives alone, in eight square rooms, all salons. There are murals, a profusion of sofas, a diffuse sensuality. Where does he eat? Where does he sleep? Finally he shows us a smaller room, with a stove-furnace and a cot. There is no more sign of running water here than in any of the other houses in Ciurea. And all these rooms, all these stage sets, what are they used for? These couches, this decor that would suit a seraglio? Since they are prohibited from wandering, now, are they trying to hold onto something of the East, through these frescos of odalisques, this harem atmosphere?

Throughout our visit, a boy dressed in blue ran before us through the streets; here and there, he would crouch down and pull out his flute, and play a weird and piercing melody.

Two miles further, the lost monastery of Bîrnova, in a fortified enclosing wall. The buildings are from the 16th century, around a massive, somber church. The monks live in autarky. We climb an external wooden staircase to a large kitchen, where a stew is simmering on the stove. Quietly, women in black are moving back and forth. There is an odor of apple and farmyard.

Next, we cross an immense forest, along a dirt road. Georges has saved his favorite spot for last, and the image will remain, for us too, one of the most precious memories of all our journeys through Romania. The road emerges in a vast meadow surrounded by trees; we leave the car and continue by foot. Horses and cows are feeding freely in this clearing. At the very end is a village, Dobrovats, preceded by a hermitage whose square bell-tower stands over the pastures and the corn fields. It's a countryside of gently rolling hills. A few monks still live in the small monastery. The church with the wide roof, painted inside with tall, dark figures, stands in the center of the enclosure as though it had fallen from the sky. Isolation, beauty, simplicity: the prototype, the pure idea of a sanctuary. Georges says he comes here whenever he feels a need for renewal, and it is true that few places in the world offer such complete harmony.

As evening comes on, the clearing comes to life. Carts loaded with corn come back to the village, a herd of 150 cows (according to the herdsmen of this collective livestock) crosses a river at a ford, heading toward the cattle sheds. Patriarchal values, and a great softness and cordiality. There is nothing to say about this picturesque hideaway; nothing to be said about it at all, if you want o stay away from clichés.

In Iaşi, Georges takes us along to dinner at the best restaurant in the city, Trei Sarmale, where the speciality is indeed sarmale (rice and ground meat wrapped in cabbage or grape leaves), served three (trei) apiece. There's a surprise at dessert: finally, a delicious cake, the *papanash*, whose substance and form are worthy of its dramatic name. It is a kind of fritter, soaked in jam and coated with cream, a compromise between the pastry of Central Europe and oriental sweets.

The following morning, we visit the Jewish cemetery, on a hill, a splendid site. The tombs are laid out in rows in the grass; made of a long, convex stone, they look like strange cylindrical logs. The oldest part of the cemetery contains many inscriptions written in German. *Hier ruhet Frau Adele Steinberg.* The most modern part is shaded by tall chestnut trees. The tombs here are marked by vertical stele. *Aci zace scumpul tata*: Here lies our dear father. *Tata*, the affectionate word for father, in Romanian. The large Jewish community of yesteryear suffered an appalling massacre in 1941. 15,000 victims, according to George. On several tombs, beside the date of death (1941), I read, between brackets, a simple word recalling the genocide: pogrom.

Then we take the road toward Braïla. Some forty miles from Iaşi, we come to the curious village of Soleshti, which clings to a steep slope and seems to stand upright by miracle. The roads are more like dirt tracks, gullied and dusty. All the cottages are thatched, and are surrounded by green and blue walls, like palisades. Ears of corn rise in small mountains in front of the doors, and in the courtyards, corn leaves are spread on the ground as litter for the geese. Sheepskins dry on the steep-pitched roofs. The peasants are wary. Since they consider their place too poor to be beautiful, they suspect us of being government officials, inspectors or tax assessors.

Is this the type of village that Ceausescu razed? Next, we go by some strange developments of very recent construction: square little houses, out of hardened clay, some still not finished, all similar (contrary to Romanian tradition). The white crossbars of the windows constitute the only ornament.

At a crossroads close to Dragusheni, the bus shelter is decorated with naive frescos. A hunter is depicted on one side, sitting on a tree trunk, reading the newspaper; on the other side, a young shepherd plays the flute — nostalgia for the pastoral world and an awakening of the political conscience. Enescu's *doïna* and Iliescu's speeches: who will have the last word in Moldova?

BRAÏLA

In Panaït Istrati's Day

Braïla stands on a rise overlooking the Danube. The vast central plaza, formerly named for Lenin, today for the Union (of Moldova and Tara Romaneasca, two principal regions), is bordered by the hideous Trajan Hotel that, nevertheless, retains a faint easygoing oriental charm. Further along, the city park stretches above the river. The view is admirable. As in Benares, and Nizhni Novgorod, the city is built only on one side. The right bank, the opposite shore, remains undeveloped: not a house, not a light post, no trace of man. A thick forest comes down to a narrow fringe of sand at the edge of the water. There must be a road of some kind, between the trees, for we can see a rudimentary ferry, impelled by a thin vapor struggling across the river, wavering in the current, and unloading and taking on cars. Otherwise, there's not much going on at the port, just a few cargo liners at anchor. Under the terrace, abandoned barges and rusted cranes, some shaky floating docks attached to the bank are the last to bear witness that this was once a flourishing place of commerce.

The Park of Braïla is interesting for a different reason. It is there that the young Adrian Zograffi, rebelling against his mother who had reproached him for courting a simple servant, met, on the walkway that overlooks the Danube, a man sitting on a bench and smoking in the dark. He was called Stavro, he was a vendor and a barman. This was the starting point of one of the most beautiful literary adventures of this century since, through the character of Adrian Zograffi, the novelist Panaït Istrati put himself into the story, and this, his first book, ensured him an international reputation.

Born in Braïla in 1884, in an old house that is no longer standing, of a Greek smuggler whom he never met and a Romanian peasant woman who worked as a laundress for two francs per day to raise her single son, Istrati represents a type of writer like the Russian Gorky and the Americans Jack London and John Steinbeck. He left school at twelve years. Self-taught, a vagrant as much by temperament as by need, he tried all the manual trades: pastrycook, farm worker, ditch digger, stevedore, ironmonger, mechanic, deliveryman, house painter, and on and on.

One evening in the spring of 1907, he arrived in Alexandria, Egypt, via Naples. After having dined on a piece of bread and cheese, he had nothing left but twelve piastres (25 cents). He saw beside him a poor devil, in even worse condition and famished, who wanted to sell him a book so that he could get a meal. The deal is done: it is Tolstoy's *Resurrection*, bought for 15 cents. Panaït started reading it at once. At midnight, the cabaret closed. With 10 cents left, he could no longer rent a room. He went out into the street and, while the cops (who would have arrested him for vagrancy), continued reading, from one reverberation to another. The rain started to fall. By early morning, soaked, frozen, he lay at the edge of the Nile, in the grass behind a sugar cane hedge, and finished the novel. Such were the universities of this star who had no other mentors but his guardian angel, his sense of smell, and above all, his courage, his vitality.

After traversing half of the countries of the Middle East, this stowaway of the cargo compartments washed up in Geneva where, at the end of his strength and resources, he wrote in his best, if approximate, French (a language he had learned on his own) a 20-page letter to Romain Rolland, who was at the time the most admired writer of the poor and the marginal (the opposite of "the littératurier"). The letter was returned to him, marked: "Left without leaving forwarding address." A year and half later, in January 1921, Istrati, passing through Nice, slit his throat in a park. The letter to Romain Rolland was found in his pocket, and this time it was delivered. Rolland, "seized with the tumult of genius," wanted to meet the desperado (who had been saved). He encouraged him to write, and in 1923 this was the foundation stone of an important *œuvre*,* his first and most beautiful book, *Kyra Kyralina*, which opens on the scene of the Park of Braïla between Adrian, the unstable teenager attracted by adventure, and Stavro, "a figure who used to be well-known in the shady side of town."

Stavro is an ambiguous character, a two-sided being, one "true" and one that "cheats;" we will learn his secret later. He persuades the young boy to go along with him, as his assistant-pastrycook, to a fair where he intends to sell lemonade. And off they go, in a cart; during the trip Stavro starts to tell him of his childhood.

When he was eight or nine years old, he lived with its mother and his elder sister Kyra in a house at the edge of the Danube. The two women spent their mornings dressing and applying their make-up, and the rest of the day they danced together and received their gallant admirers, the *moussafirs*, who came several at a time, and sang and serenaded them with guitars. They were young and handsome, elegant, with pointed moustaches; they exuded an aroma of almond oil scented with musk. Their courtship, delicate and assiduous, remained purely platonic, in spite of the ardor that enflamed the two women and threw them, all exalted after the dance, onto the thick cushions of the salon, in a perfume of aromatics and fine liquors. Most of this time, the father and the elder son, cartwrights, lived in their workshop at the other end of the city. From time to time they would descend upon the women's house. And then it was a rout. The gallants would jump out the window and slide down the bank to the Danube, leaving the brutes to beat Stavro's mother and sister mercilessly. The hapless females had only one concern: to protect their faces and their eyes. For them, the sole joy in life was to receive their admirers, and for this they patiently endured the violence of their males, as long as their beauty was not marred.

Such was the souped-up version of Braïla, during the years known elsewhere as La Belle Epoque: odalisques lounging on scented poufs, cologne-scented gents who would flee at the first alarm, and hefty men imposing their virility with blows of the fist and stick. As for the young Dragomir (Stavro being his Turkish name, adopted later on), he would stand watch, storing up memories that later on would make this chapter a full-flavored evocation of oriental ways, and would make Panaït Istrati, his confidant, the only French-speaking storyteller who could resuscitate the heady charm and the naive ostentation of *A Thousand and*

Danube at Braïla (F.F.)

One Arabian Nights.

One day, the tormenters went after them with more than their usual vigor. They put out the mother's eye, disfiguring her beautiful face. That was the end of the dancing and the parties. The two women and Dragomir fled, and the mother separated from her children with this advice: "You, Kyra, if — as it seems to me — you do not feel called to live in virtue, in that virtue that comes from God and is practiced joyfully — then do not be one of those virtuous people, dry and constrained, do not mock the Lord, and rather be what he intended you to be: be a sensualist, even a debauchee, but a debauchee with heart and soul! It's better that way. And you, Dragomir, if you cannot be a virtuous man, be like your sister and your mother, be a robber, even, but a robber who has heart, for the man without heart, my children, is a death that prevents those who are alive from living, like your father. . ." This passage summarizes Istrati's view. Love, and do as you are called to do, according to the word of St. Augustine.

The two children take refuge where they can, in abandoned cottages, helping the gleaners to gather the corn, the old women to collect the flecks of wool left on the thistles by the thousands of ewes wandering the uncultivated lands. Having known only the sheltered pleasures of the maternal salon, they discover the pleasures of the open air, "where the body bathes in the caresses of the wind that blows across a field in summer," the music of the invisible cricket orchestrating his rhythm with the distant pipe of the shepherd, the maneuvers of the bee going back and forth among the flowers, her legs dusted with pollen. In 1928, in *The Thistles of Baragan,* Istrati amplifies this anthem to nature and the Danubian landscapes in lyric terms.

A wealthy Turk notices the children, invites them to go on his sailing ship, gives them a ride along the Danube and then, having gained their confidence, takes them along to Istanbul, where he delivers Dragomir's sister to the prison depths of a harem.

Thus begins a new series of adventures for the boy, who now has to manage on his own. He is fifteen years old. Sometimes wise old men offer him good advice; more often, swindlers rob him. It turns out that the Turks like boys, too. Finally, providence sends him old Barba Yani, an itinerant vendor of *salep* (a hot drink containing flour), who becomes a true friend. "I never met but one, and that was Barba Yani. But one friend was enough to enable me to bear my misfortunes and, often, to bless life and sing its praises. For the kindness of just one man is stronger than the spite of a thousand; evil dies as soon as it is expressed, but goodness continues to radiate ever after. Like the sun that disperses the clouds and brings back joy to the earth, Barba Yani struck down the evil that was corroding my soul, and filled my heart with health."

A simplistic bit of Gospel? Here we return to the tricky side of Stavro, who now seduces Adrian. Writing in 1923, the years of Proust and Gide, Istrati finds a third way of depicting homosexuality, neither as a sulfurous hell, nor a sweet paradise, but as a natural and innocent extension of friendship. Condemnable, certainly, but more because of the hostility of public opinion than because of any inherent evil. Often, in its later novels, it evokes this intermediate zone of the feelings between the impassioned friendship and the physical contact. From these examples, the mother's advice to Dragomir and Kyra, and the acceptance of the carnal component of friendship, one foresees what Istrati brought to French literature: the poetry of ambivalence, the lyricism of promiscuity. In these novels, you feel as though you are wandering through an oriental bazaar; the world is conceived without geographical borders nor moral barriers — an open literature. French travelers have a goal, a route; they carry their identity with them and return to their starting point, enriched but not transformed. Istrati's characters leave, never to return; they lose their identity. Romanian, Greek, Turkish and Russian, they do not know who they are and allow themselves to be shaped by the adventures, the meetings, the emotions, the music and the odors they encounter. Brancusi's "Endless Column," which we will see in Tirgu Jiu, has no other principle but this rejection of limits, the bewildered desire to imbue oneself, *hic et nunc,* in the eternity of movement.

"To be a brother to the world," that is the desire of these wandering Romanians. Disdain for money and a bourgeois lifestyle, a resistance to settling down, nomadism, the aspiration to share "the grandeur of life" without worrying about a career or security, Adrian's creed, sketched with a lighter hand, precedes (minus the heavy philosophy that weighs it down) that which later became the mythology of the Hermann Hesse novels that became popular among hippies in the 1960's. Adrian's mother looks a little askance at this "duckling" who sails with such ease "in the pure water of idealism" spells out to her the articles of his catechism: "to love the letters and arts; to enjoy the terrestrial beauties; not to take join those who crush men; therefore to be satisfied materially with the bare essentials; to live in justice and fraternity; to adore a dear friend; to do as much good as possible around oneself. . ." *(Mikhaïl)*. Where are women, in all this? Adrian leaves them out, not through misogyny — there is no more beautiful portrait of a woman than that of Kyra Kyralina — but because marriage always involves restraining oneself, and egotism, and the humdrum of routine. For Istrati, the truth lies in perpetual availability. The man who has attained wisdom understands that "possession is not holding; it is perhaps to some extent in the vibrating satisfaction for which one has fought so hard, but it is all, all in fully-felt desire, the great call of life," *(Tsatsa-Minnka)*.

And again: the strength of the Romanians, one reads in a volume of memoirs *(The Pilgrim of the Heart)*, consists in being unfaithful, as worthy descendants of Trajan. "The more unfaithful one is, the more generous one is, for the unfaithful keeps nothing for himself. He fertilizes life and goes on. In him, nothing is stagnation; it's all a storm, a creative storm." After all, this was the creed of the great libertines of history: *Chi a una sola è fedele, verso l'altre è crudele (Don Giovanni)*. Aristocrats and plebeians both hate middle-class comfort.

Istrati's writing style reflects this broad, elastic concept of existence: supple sentences from which the rhythmic chant of the tale arises, in a conversational tone, the good-natured feeling of a story being told, a magical incantation, the opposite of the dense, turgid style of Cioran. Two classically Romanian authors, no doubt, but one can measure, in their disparate styles, the gulf that separates Moldova, which opens on the Danube, the Black Sea, and the orient, from the Transylvanian, taking refuge in his circle of mountains.

Istrati paid dearly for his independence of mind. Between October 1927 and February 1929, a recognized writer but still cherishing in the bottom of his heart his youthful revolt against big shots of any kind, he visited the USSR, then seen as the fatherland of workers and the Mecca of the disinherited. How his faith and his hope were transmuted into tragic disappointment, he related in the three volumes of *Toward the Other Flame*, written with collaboration with Victor Serge and Boris Souvarine and published in 1929.

Corruption, denunciations, "oppression from above" exerted by the Party, abuse of power, denials of justice, deportations (if not by absolutism, then by an all-powerful bureaucracy), the tyranny of the police force and the censors: he denounced the evils of the communist society with all the more eloquence since he had placed all his hopes in the victory of the proletariat. His work is one long indictment, increasingly feverish as it goes along.

This proud diatribe was among the first of its kind. Seven or eight years before Gide, thirty or forty years before Solzhenitsyn, Istrati detailed the vices of the Soviet dictatorship with an exceptional clarity and a courage that make these books a pleasure to read even today. Since he was only a simple vagrant, coming from a country with no international audience, no one listened. His friends turned their backs to him; the "fellow travelers" vilified him as a traitor; Romain Rolland, the venerated master, who had advised to him not to publish *Toward the Other Flame*, (in order not to give weapons to "the reaction") broke off with him. He returned to Romania in 1930, where the local authorities accused him of communist propaganda, while the fascistic groups attacked him in the bookshops where he was signing his books. All this time, in the West, the Leftist press showered him with insults and Henri Barbusse trailed him in the mud. There is no doubt that this lynching contributed to ruin the health of a man who had been undermined since adolescence by tuberculosis. He died in Bucharest, April 16, 1935, at the age of fifty-one, and was buried in the main cemetery of Belu.

Braïla Today

What remains of Istrati's Braïla? The city is nestled in a natural amphitheater, and is built in a fan shape. The streets are laid out concentrically, starting and ending at the Danube. The communist regime tore down the old town center and put up enormous concrete buildings, preceded by monumental staircases that go down to the river. The poetic disorder of yesteryear has been replace by the functional stiffness of the new puritans. In the same way, it seems that the cosmopolitan population of Greeks, Turks, and "doleful young women, timid because they are loved so tyrannically," has disappeared. Here, as elsewhere in Romania, the fight for survival has eliminated the voluptuous atmosphere that imbues the first chapters of *Kyra Kyralina*.

However, the charm of the orient still hovers over Eminescu Street, straight, commercial and pedestrian, as well as in what is left of the old maze of sinuous side streets. Behind Union Plaza is what used to be the wealthy district, and several beautiful houses remain, decorated with bas-reliefs and carved lintels. Dilapidated, dethroned, they emerge from a tumble of greenery. "As an errand boy for all kinds of shops, I often forgot myself, while making my rounds, under the windows of a house where a piano was being played. And there, I would ease my passion, my madness and my dreams that were not yet fulfilled. Often, at night I would lay down my basket outside, and go into the courtyard, climb the woodwork, and peer in through the window to see whether the pianist was as lovely as I imagined she might be." (Thus he wrote in that first letter to Romain Rolland, which was delivered a year and a half later).

In the more modest districts, the dwellings are all of the same type: a residential building facing the street, decent-looking, whitewashed in yellow or green, and, beside the façade (which does not have a door), a wall with a doorway leading to an interior court. The further into the courtyard one goes, the less tidy things look. The lawn and shrubs give way to a vacant lot littered with detritus.

Rubinelor Street, like all the others, curves between two lines of multicolored façades. Broken-up pavement, flaking walls, rickety fences. Coming back to his birthplace in 1930, Istrati found that little had changed in forty years. "The same mud pits, the same sharp stones that seem intentionally set to cut your feet or twist your ankle, especially when you are feeling your way along at night. The electric light, always half-hearted. The perennially stinking drain. And water, at night, is available only if by chance there is fire somewhere in the city," *(Pilgrim of the Heart)*.

65 years later, one can say that the situation has still not improved; but neither has it gotten worse. At No. 4, Rubinelor Street, a half-drunk man invites us into the courtyard. We are immediately surrounded by women and children. The camera seems to make them wary, at first: in these times of privatization and expropriation, mightn't we be agents come to make life difficult? Then, giving up their fears,

they let us look around, but they remain reserved. There is no water in the houses. They get it from a pump in the courtyard.

The Hotel Belvedere, where we are staying, is one of those regular and severe masonries built by the Communists to fight the insouciant anarchy of the old days. But its location, on a hilltop overlooking the majestic Danube, is incomparable, both for the unique beauty of the panorama and the constantly changing spectacle. Nothing could be more alive or merrier than the animation along the riverbank. We go down the concrete staircase. No cars are at the bottom; the path is reserved, for a mile or two, to pedestrians and cyclists. Just below the hotel, a swimming hole is separated from the walkway by a simple net. "Reserved for those under fifteen years," the sign says. On this sunny afternoon late in September, ten young boys are playing in the water, frolicking and enjoying their freedom. The triumph and glory of nature.

At twilight, the scene changes. Couples walk down from the city and sit at the river's edge. This is the young people's meeting place. Children, teenagers swim in the Danube, with no apparent concern for its yellow color; and some wash with soap (for good reason) but then jump back into the dubious water for a rinse. We sat on the floating dock and enjoyed the spectacle until nightfall, listening to the powerful current of the Danube, mingled with the laughter and the murmurs of the young people, happy, free, relaxed. Perhaps the old pleasure that suffused Braïla survives in these watery and naturalist rites.

A terrace over the river enhances the rooms of the Belvedere Hotel. By what aberration is the breakfast room stuck in cave, without view, without air? Backed against a concrete pillar, you choke down a bad coffee. Another sign of the peasants' lack of pragmatism and their fatalistic attitude comes up when we set out for Tulcea, on the other side of the Danube, by ferry. Not the tiny ferry that we saw from our windows, but the big ferry that departs from Comorofca, a rundown district of huts and shacks, the most miserable neighborhood in Braïla (already in Istrati's day — his mother had to move there, to save a bit on the monthly rent).

We reach the embankment. There are two lines of vehicles: "normal," a mob of broken-down cars and several hours' wait; and "priority," for the *nomenklatura* and diplomatic plates. We are the first to be embarked. And thus, on the other side of the river, the first to be unloaded. It is here that the difficulties start. The ferry is loaded with trucks so heavy that it is riding well below the level of the unloading dock. We are at least 18 inches too low. Svetlana, who is driving our Peugeot that day, is a lovely young Romanian, very beautiful, very elegant. She immediately realizes that it is impossible to get across. "Try it anyway!" the dockers advise her, in the uncooperative attitude typical of peasant conservatism. Svetlana gets out of the car and apostrophizes them in their own language. They bring two beams, but lay them down on the ferry one beside the other, so that they are of no help whatsoever. Then the young woman, bending down and moving the beams herself, arranges them to form two steps. The strapping men, stunned, look on without saying anything, without making a single gesture, as this Venus in a fine leather coat moves everything into place. She gets back behind the wheel and succeeds in getting the car out.

In this field too, nothing has changed for 65 years. Istrati wrote of a certain Mr. Wolff, chief engineer of Braïla docks, that "he is highly skilled and is one of the rare Germans who have not been replaced by Romanian sinecurists, as has become common since it became fashionable to think that they can get along without Germans. They are getting along without them, but the results are lamentable. Everywhere is bureaucracy, waste, plundering, ineptitude."

An eternal reigns between the Germanic efficiency and the oriental negligence, Between West and East. Or North-South? In Kishinau, we saw that 70% of the Romanians leave the economic and political power in the hands of the 30% of Russians — one wonders how much of that is the result of Moscow's domination and how much is the result of natural inclinations. After Karol Hohenzollern took the Romanian crown in 1866, the German influence was stronger. The commercial docks and grain silos in Braïla were built by the Germans, with the promise that better shipping conditions would "put butter on everyone's spinach;" instead, it gave more butter to those who already had some, and put the rest out of work. For years, the grain elevators that replaced hundred of laborers had to be guarded with guns and bayonets.

Nostalgia for the old ways versus the military organization of the silos. The Germans left, eventually, and the elevators remained, but the Romanians avenge themselves for this necessary concession to the everyday rules of commerce by preserving an antiquated ferry and methods of unloading that are as picturesque as they are inoperative.

* *Folio*, No. 1253. Joseph Kessel republished Istrati's romantic *œuvre*, at Gallimard (1968-1970), in four volumes. *Les Cahiers Panaït Istrati* regularly publishes documents and letters. Volume 2/3/4 (1987) contains all his correspondence with Romain Rolland.

The Danube Delta

Tulcea, at the mouth of the delta, embodies all the ugliest features of communist town planning: as if, before yielding to this immense dissolution of nature in a marsh as big as half of Corsica, man, little man wanted to affirm one more time his power, by pouring tons of proletarian concrete. Fortunately, there are plenty of boats to brighten up the port. Moored at the quays, bobbing on the dark water, are skiffs of every size and shape, generally in a state of decay.

When we first visited, in 1990, Mr. Giorgescu organized a two-hour excursion for us. He calls himself the director of the French Navigation Company on the Danube, an antique company that still has five tug boats, five barges, and a tanker ship, all dating back to before the war of 1914. Coal has simply been replaced by fuel oil. We go by motorboat, with only one man as crew. This boat seems less prehistoric, and cuts a straight path for the arm of Sulina, where a canal was carved in 1900 to cut the delta in half and allow direct access to the sea. The two other arms of the Danube, Chilia to the north, bordering on the Ukraine, and Saint-George to the south, enclose within their arabesques a triangle of 1700 miles, inhabited by some 25,000 islanders and fishermen and millions of fish and birds.

By a secondary channel that curves between willows and reeds, we go toward the *Bratul Chilia* and return to Tulcea via Ismaïl, a Ukrainian port. It is too late in the season (late October): the migratory birds have flown away, and we did not see any of the pelicans, ducks, cranes, wild geese, swans, herons and storks that our host describes to us in wondering tones. The reeds stretch as far as the eye can see, under an already chilly sky.

We stop briefly in the tiny village of Patlageanca, just a few thatched houses at the edge of the river. A woman shows us a seven month old calf; then a peasant invites us into his place: a tiny farm inside a palisade fence. Goats, pigs, hens. The house has a single room, furnished with a big bed with a black and white cover, and a clay hearth, which is used as both cooking stove and furnace. In a lean-to shed, the peasant invites us to drink some of his wine. Just at that moment his wife, who has been to a wedding, brings in a kind of kugelhopf, a treasure that she absolutely insists on sharing with us. They store their corn in a very tall and very narrow hut, built on pilings and guarded by a dog on a chain.

This turns out to be our most beautiful memory from our first foray to the delta: the feeling of a life apart, and some isolated survivors at the end of the universe. They remain, forgotten by everyone, descendants of fugitives and outlaws who found refuge in the last century between the open arms of the Danube; and they have transformed their criminal past into patriarchal dignity. Does the Romanian name for the Danube, *Dunârea*, in its liquidy intonations, give a better sense of a fragile world, in perpetual flow? We like to think that convicts, deserters, Turkish and Russian outcasts, fugitives of all types landed here like migratory birds, in the midst of the marshes, where the river that has watered those cities loaded with history (Ulm, Ratisbon, Vienna, Bratislava, Budapest, Belgrade), that has fertilized the most famous civilizations and federated by its majestic course the great cultures of Europe, serves in the end as shelter for an ill-defined tribe of wanderers, of pariahs.

Sic transit gloria mundi, but without the visions of skeletons and monsters, as in the macabre paintings of Valdés Leal in Seville; with, on the contrary, a softness, a calm and philosophical beauty, a quiet obviousness, as if it were natural that the immense Danube, tired from having to change its name seven times according to the countries it crosses or skirts (only the name "Danube" does not occur along its actual path) and nourished by the thought of so many great men born along its

banks, agreed to provide, on the last of its 1600 miles a no man's land for the stray sons of God.

The second time we visited (September 1992), we spent the whole day on the delta thanks to the vice-governor, who put his boat at our disposal. According to him, the SFN has gone out of business. We set out along the canal Mila 35, navigating close to the banks, between sand bars and bull rushes. Here in the marshes, a few humps of dry land are isolated among streams and mud ponds, swathes of tall grasses stand knee-deep in the water, and a labyrinth of rivulets and tributaries scattered between the reeds form a primordial landscape. It calls to mind the fabulous time when the waters were not yet separated from the earth, when there was only an immense muddy agglomeration of silt, grasses and vegetable matter. A vulture, a cormorant, and two swans fly away suddenly as we round a bend. A heron inspects his elegant reflection in a pool. Mr. Ioan Munteanu, a biologist, tells us about the riches of the delta, a paradise for botanists and zoologists. The vice-governor's flat-bottomed boat requires only three feet of water, so we can venture into narrow passages and go up close to the rustling banks. No landscape could hint more strongly of an invisible fauna than this quivering watery labyrinth.

We are unexpectedly reminded of civilization. Anchored across the river, on a boat the same size as ours, a half-dozen people are sitting in the sun, chatting. On the rear deck, turned toward the middle of the current, sits a priest in a black cassock and hat, large and bearded. He is fishing. Mr. Munteanu tells our pilot to turn around and pull up close to the boat: he has recognized two daughters of King Michael of Romania: Sophie, in black, and Marie, in a blue and black sweater. We go on board. Introductions. They speak excellent French. Raised in Switzerland, they hardly speak Romanian, and their father is much faulted for this. Their ignorance of the national language is an additional argument against the restoration of the monarchy. They are here because of the alarming state of the delta: half of the flora and fauna have disappeared, killed by pollution. How can this disaster be repaired? They seem concerned, sincere, and unaffected.

As for the priest, he is interested in nothing but politics. He asks me whether I plan to talk about the "spiritual life" in my book on Romania. Have I met with the bishops? Cloying, talkative, an intriguer, he makes me think of Rangoni in *Boris Godunov,* the Jesuit who pushes Marina to mount the throne of Russia in order to convert the orthodox to the true religion. Although this is a simple priest from the Stavropoulos church in Bucharest, he plays an important role with the royal family. It is he who organized the deposed sovereign's last visit (a complete fiasco) to Romania. He is called Justin, and he shamelessly envelopes the usual arguments of the far Right in mystical clouds.

Apparently to convince the princesses that he supports their ecological crusade, he disguised himself, that day, as a fisherman. "The real problem of the Danube," Mr. Munteanu told us later, "is not pollution but the lowering of the water level for ten years, which has upset the ecological balance." And who told the princesses about the pollution? Father Justin, it seems.

We take a stopover at Mila 23 (23 miles from the sea), in a village of Lipovenes. They can be recognized by the two onion domes, quite

Danube Delta: Mila 23

Slavic, of their wooden and sheet metal church, as well as from the bright blond hair of the children. The Lipovenes, or Lippovinians, arrived from Russia in the 18th century. They practiced a heresy that was persecuted by the authorities. Their name comes from the fact that they kneel only before icons made out of lime wood *(lippa)*. They reject the priesthood, the sacraments, marriage and military service, and they are subdivided into several sects: the *Popovitsy* (who accept priests), the *Bezpopovitsy* (who challenge them), the Molokhans (who drink milk — *molokho* is Russian for milk) and the *Skoptsy* (who castrate themselves). At least, that is how it used to be. They have settled down somewhat, and rejoined the orthodox liturgy. Their costumes and their gestures are suffused with a primitive paganism. How can you not become a great admirer of nature, when you live in isolation, removed from history and the lives of other men, between heaven and water?

Their first church was flooded in 1970, and was abandoned. Built of wood, it is still standing and appears solid, wallowing in a hollow in the ground, like Noah's Ark come to rest. We go in through a window, following a young boy with blue eyes and hair as yellow as corn. He climbs the rafters and startles us by flushing out a dove that he's found there. Petrika, a cherubic jokester, must be a descendant of the Molokhans, his velvety skin is so opalescent.

Green fences divide the village into small yards. Made of unfired clay and corrugated metal, but clean and well-maintained, the little houses have only one room. The kitchen and the bathroom are adjoined, so they can be heated by the same stove. A couple invites us in and offers us a taste of crayfish. The only occupation is fishing. Fish-drying equipment is leaned up against the houses, along with racks for storing the trays and the stakes with which they build weirs, since the ice of winter would damage them and the high waters of spring would carry them away. Next, we go into an old woman's home. She has a wall-hanging with a gallant scene decorating her wall, between two antique icons. She speaks only Russian, laughs all the time, and takes pride in showing us the sauna that has been built in her bathroom. The fire is fed with reeds. She pours some boiling water on the coal and giggles. Hens are walking about in her yard. She gets by quite well, this old woman who dries and salts carp for a living. She even has electricity; she has several ceiling lights.

If the delta as a whole gave us the impression of an archaic world, in this village we encountered a fragment of humanity that goes back to the days of Genesis. Wood, mud and straw, a minimal existence but unquestionably a happy one. The hamlet has no other name than the bureaucratic "Mila 23." Indeed, it hardly exists; it was dropped there by chance, and it seems as though it could set out again down the current and wash up further along between other willows, other reeds. In front of every house, a boat is ready. The children go to the school by rowboat, just as they do along the Amazon. Everything is unstable, precarious, horizontal, fleeting, and with a primordial, timeless beauty.

We lunch at Lebada, in a "tourist complex" worthy of the name. Grilled *somn*, which is an excellent sort of catfish, which may be caught year-round (like perch and pike). For the other species, zander, bream, carp (some carp weigh 25 pounds and are over a yard long), tench, sterlet, and sturgeon, fishing is regulated.

We head back via the *Bratul* Sulina; Mr. Munteanu is standing forward, up in the bow, observing the sky. Just as we are passing between two lakes, Obretinu *Mare* ("large": from the Lating "*magnus*") on the right and Obretinu *Mic* ("small") on the left, he suddenly turns to us with excitement. At the horizon, we see the silhouette of a huge flock of birds, long rows of them: the famous pelicans of the delta. They pass overhead in successive waves and then land next to Obretinu Mic, at the end of a long stretch of dry land. "What a spectacle!" our enthusiastic guide exclaims. "I've only seen such a huge flock once or twice in my life!" We beach the boat and walk about half a mile over cracked, dry mud to get closer to the birds gathered at the edge of the lake.

Mr. Munteanu estimates there are 5,000 of them, maybe half of all the pelicans in the reserve. And he explains the problem they create. There are some 5,000 nests, that is to say 10,000 adults, plus the young, one or two per pair, which can be recognized by their black wings which later turn white. The pelicans live in colonies; each bird weighs up to 60 lbs.. They stand three feet tall, with a six foot wingspan. We advance cautiously. They stand by the water's edge, motionless, in tight rows; one or two take off, with no sign of their ponderous weight. An adult — and here is the problem — eats eight pounds of fish per day. That comes to 35 tons daily for the whole colony. Add to that what the 50,000 cormorants consume. The birds of the delta eat as much fish as the Romanians, between 4,000 and 5,000 tons per annum.

And — to make matters worse — a bird that eats nothing but fish is not edible by humans. What to do? Keep these gluttons that, given the water conditions and the diminishing supply of fish, threaten the food supply of an already underfed population? Or destroy their nests? The Ukrainians to the north and the Bulgarians to the south have eliminated their pelican colonies; only Romania continues to put up with them — an astonishing example of generosity for a regime that was known to be more pragmatic than romantic.

> *When the pelican, wearied from her long flight,*
> *Returns to the rushes at the fall of night...*

The verses of *The Night of May* echo in the memory of any French schoolchild, but if things worked the way the poet imagined, the problem would not exist. Musset believed that the pelican tore its own heart with its beak to nourish its young with its entrails:

> *On its feast of death it subsides and staggers,*
> *Drunk with pleasure, tenderness and horror.*

The reality is quite different. The pelican collects up to fifteen pounds of fish in the sac in its throat, which it chews before passing them on to the chicks in the nest. If this bird with the portable pantry senses danger, it regurgitates the contents and flies away. Obretinu Mic attracted these thousands of birds because it is so shallow, and concentrates in its water a maximum of fish, whereas the lake opposite, larger but deeper, would require more work. Greedy, lazy, pragmatic are these birds; but of a royal splendor that justifies the reveries of poets.

Danube Delta: Pelicans

THE BLACK SEA

Why "black"? The Ancients called this the *Pontus Euxinus*, that is to say "the hospitable." By antiphrasis, for, since time immemorial, this inland sea has been feared for its storms; and "black" signifies danger-ous, threatening, oppressive. Its water is, in fact, no darker than that of the Mediterranean. Mircea Eliade, in one of his wonderful volumes of memoirs, *Promises of the Equinox*, tells how he and his student friends started out from Tulcea in a boat and were surprised in the open water by a hurricane. They barely avoided sinking. After a whole week, with a broken mast, exhausted, they managed to regain Constantza, Roma-nia's largest port and the capital of Dobrogiea. This area, which ex-tends from the right bank of the Danube to the coast, was under Turk-ish control until 1878.

"Black." How far back does this name date? The Ottoman occupa-tion, of sinister memory? Or far earlier, at the time of Dacia and the Ro-man colonization? Constantza was used as a place of exile for Romans who fell into disgrace: it was the Siberia of the Urbs. The poet Ovid was the most famous victim of this dark fate. It is hard to say why the Emperor Augustus punished so harshly the inoffensive author of *Loves* and *Metamorphoses*. Ovid languished for nine years and died, in 17 AD, in

Constanţa: Casino interior. Verso: general view

the city that was called at that time "Tomis," from the Greek and meaning, "separate pieces, portions" (cf. English "tome," an individual
volume). This name also seems to reflect the legend, "black" indeed,
according to which Medea, the princess of Colchid (an area bordering
the eastern shore of the *Pontus Euxinus*) dismembered her brother Ab-
syrte.

It is well known how hard the Communists tried to break the
"black magic" spell that holds their single warm water port under its
noxious charm, which has been reduced to little but a land of loneliness, exile and terror, an inhospitable, even barbarian zone. They
transformed this formerly wild coast into seaside resorts, lined with
pseudo-luxury hotels, factitious cheerfulness and vacation camps.
Panaït Istrati described Dobrogiea, as a hostile steppe swept by the icy
wind of winter, then glazed by the kiln of summer — and moreover, it
is here that Marshal Antonescu's fascistic government deported the
Gypsies, and the People's Democracy of 1945 deported the Romanian

Black Sea: Eforie resort

Black Sea: Venus/Aurora resort

Germans. But then, from Mamaia to Mangalia, the east coast became the destination for a far sweeter form of deportation: this was the chosen vacation spot, in vast "tourist complexes," for worthy workers, Party chiefs, the regime's favorites and the representatives of the European Communist Parties, who found here beaches and sun at ridiculously low prices.

An active port shipping grains and petroleum, Constantza (renamed for the sister of Emperor Constantine) also receives Russian boats that come for the granite of Dobrogiea, which paves the streets not only of Braïla and Bucharest, but of Odessa, Tbilisi and Sevastopol. The city where he is buried (although no one has been able to locate his grave) has not forgotten Ovid. His statue stands in the central square, and on its base are the four lines in Latin that Ovid had composed as his epitaph.

Tenerorum lusor amorum, "the one who sings of tender loves," he characterized himself. There isn't much left, in modern Constantza, of the delicate eroticism that wafts through his poetry, except, perhaps, in the archaeological museum (but sheltered, precisely, in a museum), where some ancient statues display a disconcerting ambiguity: an Apollo with feminine features, Isis with an inviting mouth, an Eros, Bacchus, the Three Graces. . . As for the spirit of *Metamorphoses,* the only reminder is in the strange shape of a bluish marble Snake, with the head of a sheep and with human ears and hair.

The dilapidated streets have a certain charm. By the main square, one shifts abruptly from the reveries of Ovid to the chaos of the Gypsies, and the Turks who have set up a superb café-patisserie on the corner. Svetlana is convinced that they are Gypsies, too. There's quite a choice of sweets, fritters with jam, Turkish baklava with honey, Romanian placintas ("our national pastry," says Istrati, "which is nothing more than a pastry stuffed with cheese and eggs or with ground meat and onion, the whole drowned in good pork fat." This establishment, with its success and the abundance of goods, contrasts sharply with the average Romanian trade, always weak. "The Gypsies are rich," says Svetlana, who does not like them. "Before the Revolution, they organized trips abroad: every ticket cost five pounds of gold." Human flesh versus noble metal: a metamorphosis that Ovid would have appreciated. In any event, it seems to me that the poet would have loved to sit at a table in this pastry shop, and temper the bitterness of his exile with the taste of honey, poppy seeds, almond paste and figs from the oriental sweets makers.

Dinner at the House of Lions, a privately-run restaurant, with an extensive menu and very good food. The room on the main floor, softly lit and cozily decorated with carpet and dark wall-hangings, offers a good example of the Belle Epoque style, an elegant parentheses in the chronic bad luck of the Romanians. The building dates back to 1898. Is it possible that the practice of marking each building with its date of construction has to do with the need to fix times and dates in a continuously shifting and chaotic history? The casino is dated 1910. It stands on an artificial rock at the end of the peninsula that juts across the bay, close to a pleasant terraced garden. A masterpiece of Art Nouveau, covered with swirls, one of my Romanian correspondents cited it as a specimen of national baroque whereas it is only an amusing offshoot of cosmopolitan kitsch. This building intrigued us.

Constanţa: Minaret

We returned the following day morning. It was a Sunday. Young sailors were sauntering along the oceanfront. At the door of the casino, a maitre d'hotel, in a tuxedo, tries to keep us from entering. "No entry." — Why? asks Norbert. "Because it's prohibited." We go in anyway, and walk up one level (by a staircase so encumbered with mouldings, arabesques and fringes that only Theophilus Gautier could de-

scribe it). In a vast, barely-lit room (to save electricity, or to add a touch of mystique?) young people lounge on velvet seats and sip Coke, in front of a catwalk where girls are parading. There's a deafening sound system. It must be a beauty contest, or a fashion show. Unless these are the sons of Turkish pashas who have come to recruit oda-lisques for their fathers, intended for their seraglios? No one assump-

Constanţa: the port

tion is any more incongruous than the others. Is it a contest of fashions, models, in this city that is lost at the end of the world, where people dress however they can? And, even stranger, the audience is silent. Nobody applauds, no one shows any curiosity, the apathy is complete. The ceremony proceeds in a funereal environment, amidst a tumult of furniture, all decorated with frantic preciousness.

South of Constantza, Ceausescu and the dignitaries of his clan built their seaside residences, next to an entirely new village baptized Olympus. Olympus, Neptune, Venus: that is how the resorts built since the war have been named. Did the regime think that their concrete ugliness would be overlooked if they evoked the blessing of the Greek gods?

In Olympus, Ceausescu's large villa (now empty) is guarded by soldiers who cadge a cigarette from passersby. The members of Ceausescu's retinue lived in comfortable houses nearby, which can now be rented, at a relatively high price. Norbert has rented one for two days. First, we have to pick up the key at a hard-to-find address, then we have to hunt around to find the house. It has two large rooms on the ground floor, plus a room for the staff, and three rooms upstairs, two bathrooms, and, most notable, furniture, sanitary facilities, valves and fittings that are infinitely better than the usual in Romania. This is nice, almost luxurious. The rent includes the services of a cleaning lady who, as soon as she arrives, sits in front of the television and turns up the volume all the way.

Between the house and the boardwalk is a lovely little garden. There are beautiful walkways along the beach, and it's wonderful swimming, in water that is not very salty — apparently because of the constant influx from the Danube and other rivers. Large hotels are deployed all along the cliff. On the embankment, in plain view, an enormous bovine carcass is decomposing. According to Ovid, Jupiter disguised himself as a bull to abduct the young princess Europa. Is this carrion left on the shore the ultimate metamorphosis of the god, an image of Ceausescu's downfall? The "Olympian splendor"of his regime is transformed into a rotting hulk.

We had further proof that the regime left strange after-effects the following day, in a scene that made all three of us ashamed to be French.

In Mangalia, the last city on the coast before the Bulgarian border, a "French Library" was supposed to be inaugurated: a gift of France (of which France? We shall soon see), and consequently they needed an official authority to chair the ceremony. The Ambassador of France, detained by other duties, had asked Norbert to represent him.

We arrive at Mangalia: a city laid out according to a symmetrical plan, austere streets at right angles, in the fascistic style. Where is the "French Library"? Finally we get to the designated location. A little late. The ceremony has already started. Ceremony? Or farce? In a white, modern room on the ground floor of a new building, a little girl with a stupid voice struggles through a recital of "a hen on a wall" and is applauded by a circle of grandmas in floral print dresses. "Another win for French culture!" comments a self-satisfied, plump fellow who is sitting there. He speaks next.

It is Pierre Poujade. What? Poujade, as in poujadism? I rub my ears. He's the one. On a "mission." What kind of mission? He then commences, for the benefit of the grandmothers and the little girl, a speech in which he asserts that Romania is a marvelous country because the round-trip flight Paris-Constantza costs only $250, a night in a hotel $20, the best meal $5. "Take advantage!" he says. This advice could not be more absurd; actually, it is he himself whom he is congratulating for having unearthed a corner of Europe where he can get a tan, cheaply. A man representing the farm-combine and the payoff: a caricature Frenchman, in all his idiosyncrasy. All he is missing is the Basque beret and a loaf of bread. He claims to organize bus tours in France for young Romanians, with sightseeing, debates, and shows where they sing Romanian folklore. Poor Romania! Poor France! While he is praising fraternity, I step aside to examine the two thousand French books lining the walls, the gift that justified his visit.

What a horror! Besides several "classics" from Le Seuil publishers (Hugo, Balzac, Zola, Flaubert, Corneille, Molière, Montesquieu) and a series of appropriate paperbacks, the rest — four-fifths of the collection, consists of beach reading and some soppy novels that no bookseller in France would dare to put on sale. I think of the Romanians' appetite for reading; of their often perfect knowledge of the French language; of the impossibility of finding French books in the Romanian bookshops; and of the high price at which they would be sold, if any books were found. I imagine a young man coming into this "French

Library" offered by France (what he believes to be France), sponsored by a French politician; I see him combing the shelves for something new, and carrying home, as if it were a fine flower of French literature, a volume from one of these series. Won't he be turned off forever from France, and its culture?

I try to get some information. How can such an imposture be possible? To cap it all off, the Library is named for "Arthur Rimbaud." A bust of the poet is ensconced on one shelf. The librarian is a young lady who speaks French. A tourism association from the Ardennes (whence the reference to Rimbaud) had visited Mangalia a few years ago. The Frenchmen had asked this Romanian, who served as their tour guide-interpreter, what they could do to help. "Books," she answered. They collected 2,400 from all of northeastern France and sent them to her; she stored them herself, and got the town hall to donate a room; then she went to Charleville to learn the trade of librarian.

Let's go back a little further. It turns out that the tourism club used to organize cheap vacations to the country of Ceausescu for Communists from the Ardennes. After Romania's 1989 revolution, the club, directed by a trade unionist, decided to recycle itself as a "humanitarian aid" organization engaged in "cultural exchange." Mr. Pierre Poujade's crusade was grafted onto this. On the pretext of helping the Romanians to resist the consumer society, they provided a new excuse for subsidized visits! Thus the cultural rejects of the Ardennes (and the town of Villerupt in particular), thanks to the Brezhnevite coalition, flowed to the beaches of the Black Sea.

Charleville also donated some wheelchairs for the hospitals. Worn out, scratched and damaged. This donation was subsidized, too. As a result of this scam, the Sea is "blacker" than ever, since the coast is used as the dumping ground of Europe. Carrions of cattle and corpses of books.

On the road to Bucharest, we crossed the Danube at Giurgeni, on a fairly new bridge (in 1966, they still used the ferry). The toll collector asks us for the fare, but we haven't got a single *leu* left. We offer her a pack of cigarettes, and she is delighted to let us through without a ticket. Soldiers are guarding the bridge. A few cigarettes to them too, and we are allowed to photograph the river, classified as a top military-strategic site. On the other bank, a boy and girl have just caught two big fish. We buy them for three dollars. Halfway to the capital, we stop in a village that seems to come straight out of a Turgenev story: a road white with dust, wooden fences, low houses in the middle of gardens. The peasants are friendly. A woman makes us a gift of a watermelon. Her son has emigrated to China. Leaving Romania for China is like jumping from the frying pan into the fire, to quote Svetlana, who over-quotes this quote.

Then, just before Urziceni, we come upon a convoy of covered carts stretching for several miles. This is our second contact, and quite different from the first, with the world of Gypsies. Geese (stolen, according to Svetlana) are hanging in cages off the back of the wagons. Ferrante wants to photograph these proud-looking nomads dressed in their multicolored rags, so we stop at the front of the procession. The head of the household wants to be paid; we give him five dollars. The women approach, press against us, touch our pockets, and mumble something, not an inch from our faces. It's impossible to fend them off. Meanwhile, the other carts pull up; the men rush toward us, demanding money. The circle closes in, and the atmosphere gets tense; the women chant, and start rubbing against the car. It is time to give up. With all the windows rolled up, we speed away.

We often stumbled on encampments of these wanderers, above or below the road level, during the rest of our travels, especially in Transylvania, near Sighishoara, where they meet every year to elect their king. Unbridled horses graze between the tents. As soon as one stops to get a look at the splendid spectacle of these brick-hued men and women, slender, straight, lordly under their variegated garb, a swarm of children runs up at full speed to beg for cigarettes and money. Raising their skirts above their naked feet, the women try in turn. Soon they are on you, up against you, with this refined multifaceted technique, full-body contact plus an excavating caress (with such digital dexterity), the art of inspecting the contents of your pockets while hypnotizing your defense reflexes with their monotonous nasal chant. The only means of evading this soft, serpentine aggression is not very glorious; the only thing to do is to escape before the men arrive as reinforcement. They are said to be armed and quick to play with a knife: a rumor, probably, but one that hardly encourages confidence.

Coming into Bucharest from the airport, the first impression is none too prepossessing. After crossing or skirting large parks that remind us that the city was built upon the site of a forest, we came to Plaza (Piața) Romana where Magheru starts, an immense rectilinear avenue. The self-conscious and rigid ostentation is combined with the poverty of the socialist countries: how discouraging to the pedestrian, passing between two concrete cliffs, searching in vain for something cheerful to look at. The shops are empty; in the windows a can of vegetables dialogues with a jar of gherkins, and, as the only testament of an imagination strangled by fifty years of restrictions, here and there a mannequin poses in absurdly festive garb to fill the vitrine. The crowd, however, files by endlessly: this is the north-south axis of the city, which crosses the east-west axis, Gheorghiu-Dej Boulevard, at University Plaza.

The protesting miners who came from Jiu in September 1991 camped at University Plaza, in front of the Hotel InterContinental (a 1970's skyscraper); every window on the ground floor was broken, that first evening. We were coming back from a visit to Craiova, and ran into this scene. It was past midnight. The miners, dressed in khaki, with an iron bar under the arm or a sledge hammer over the shoulder, were sauntering around the deluxe hotel; they seemed rather thin and small, not the giants we would have expected. They had cobbled

Bucharest: Ceaușescu Palace

Bucharest: the old city

together some barricades on Magheru by ripping up the ironwork grids from the flowerbed along the avenue.

Some flames were burning on the roadway. In a country where everything is in short supply, this destruction is heart-wrenching. Why did they come? Why the violence? We questioned the by-standers. For economic reasons, according to some: the miners were demanding wage increases, the resignation of Mr. Roman, the Prime Minister, and the end of the austerity program. That was an alibi, oth-ers maintained: Iliescu, the disgraced president, had caused the riot in

Bucharest: the new city

an effort to get rid of Roman. Some even floated the idea of a disguised military putsch. Everywhere, it seemed, were suspicion, doubt and confusion. Two nights later, the InterContinental had been completely rehabilitated; every pane of glass was in place, shining with a new gleam; a miracle, in these times of shortage. Most of the miners, lying in the grass in front of the National Theater, slept with closed fists. Roman had announced his resignation, but continued to direct affairs. And suspicion, doubt and confusion persisted. And by contrast to the demonstrations in July 1990, this time the young people, the students (whom the miners had beaten up the first time), made a pact with the sedition. On one of the sidewalks they created a kind of altar built of cans and metal scrap, in commemoration of one of their comrades who had been killed. It's impossible to know by whom: by the black shirts from Jiu? or by the police force?

One has only to step off Magheru and cross by any of the smaller streets in the direction of Dacia Boulevard to discover a more representative Bucharest, more intimate, one that remembers its marshy and forested origins: there are trees everywhere, and gardens, and gracious houses surrounded by greenery and a maze of lanes, passages, and courtyards. Much of the construction is from the 1900's, and is still very lovely, with just enough quaint charm to miss being kitsch and evoke a palpable sense of poetry.

Strolling through this neighborhood is delectable; every corner offers a surprise, a village spared the ugliness of modern town planning. We found only one shop, and it specialized in honey and royal jelly. The merchant showed us how to mix honey with royal jelly, using only wooden or plastic implements (as metal would ruin the apiary miracle). Faith in honeybees and the virtues of their products is not a whim imported from abroad: it is part of the national culture, a vestige of Carpathian life that is mentioned in early Greek references.

That this country, prey to chronic misfortune, needs magical beliefs to survive does not astonish us. Gerovital (*Geritol* in the US), an elixir against old age invented by doctors in Bucharest, is the only Romanian specialty that credulous foreigners envy them. A pot of royal jelly, awfully small, costs $10 in Paris but in Bucharest in 1991 it

Bucharest: Cotroceni Palace, formerly the Royal Summer Palace
Overleaf: Bucharest, the Patriarchy

was 100 *lei*, or 50 cents; but that is a lot of money for a country where the average wages were around 6,000 lei at the time. The label, which was not replaced, still read 50 lei. In one year, since the price liberalization, prices had doubled. The miners (to finish with them for once and for all) were earning 15,000 lei, but they work with antiquated tools and under abominable conditions.

Dacia Boulevard is lined with old villas, with tasteful ornamentation, which serve as embassies. There is also a French Cultural Institute, opposite one of the loveliest public gardens in the city, in a palace built in 1909 by Maugsch. As in many of the private houses in Bucharest, an immense foyer takes up half the floor space and all the height, bordered on the second floor by a gallery that opens into all the other rooms. The staircase, an important decorative element, the canopies, grids, balustrades, and thousand details of wrought iron or carved wood happily evoke the decorative panache of Art Nouveau.

The Director of the establishment, which is filled with clients from the moment the doors open, invites us to his place, a few blocks away. However, he has forgotten or lost his key. At once the entire neighborhood gets involved: one will try to get in through the window. A woman brings a ladder. The woman's tenant leans out and offers advice. Frederic climbs the balcony. A man runs up with a screwdriver and talks about picking the lock. In impeccable French, he starts to tell me his whole life story, his vexations, his hopes. His father had had a house in Bessarabia (the part of Moldova that was annexed by the USSR after the war), along the Dniestr, and he had a library of sixteen thousand volumes, including some very rare books, that were carried away during the war by the Germans. He is basking in the illusion that he may recover them, now that there is talk of returning private property. How many times, during our visits, we heard people saying, "My grandfather had 800 acres of land; they are promising to give me back ten of them." While explaining to me that his ancestors were governors at the Russian court, the man with the screwdriver is supervising Frederic very closely, for neither fantasies of the past nor speculations about the future are worth losing a tool that it would be very difficult to replace.

Alex, a Romanian friend, takes us along to the Armenian neighborhood, bounded on the east by strada Galatzi, on the north by strada Shevshchenko (an extension of Dacia Boulevard), to the west by calea Moshilor, and to the south by Republicii Boulevard. The oldest house in Bucharest is known as Put Melik, on strada Spatarului. It dates back to 1740 and is built of stone, with wooden columns on the ground floor and a closed wooden veranda on the second story. Although it is currently unoccupied, it used to be a museum housing the canvases of Theodor Pallady, a painter who is highly prized in these parts. He was trained in the School of Paris at the end of the last century, and, a friend of Matisse, was an exuberant colorist. At strada Venerei, two stone sphinxes keep watch over an abandoned garden. The houses are embellished with arcades, turrets, mouldings, all a bit rundown after fifty years of neglect. There are only houses, mostly single-story, with a courtyard and garden. We did not see any shops or cafés. There is an impression that the city has fallen into a deep sleep, like in a fairy tale or a sci-fi fantasy adventure.

And adventures we did find, on strada Silvestru, on September 23, 1992. First, we met an old woman, standing on the threshold of her leprous villa; when she heard us speaking French, she insisted on inviting us in and showing us photographs of her daughter, who had emigrated to Paris. She was nearly crying, of emotion, nostalgia, impossible hopes, and dreams cherished in vain. We asked for permission to see the garden, on the other side of the house. "It is not in very good shape," she murmured, without daring to refuse our request. The garden was as dilapidated as the villa.

Three houses further along, an elegant residence with columns (no less dilapidated than the other), catches Ferrante's eye. By the rusted gate, he starts to take pictures. The house seems deserted — "unless," jokes Alex, "gypsies might have moved in." Suddenly out bursts a big, impetuous, powerfully built man, in his sixties, wearing a jacket and tie and speaking flawless French. He throws himself against the gate and screams at us with outrageous violence. "Get out of here! You are *Securitate!*" And, grabbing two bars of the gate in his meaty fists, he spits in Ferrante's face. Alex and Mihaï beckon to us to move away, without reacting. What a shock, from a carefully-dressed and cultivated man, this explosion of old racist resentments and more recent political animosity that ignite his torrent of invectives. "You are from the Securitate! You are Gypsies! You are with the French secret

Bucharest: The National Military House

service, which ruined our country!"

Alex thinks he must be a former victim of Ceausescu: the sight of a camera drives him into a panic, making him think he is being tailed again. Another hypothesis: he might be renting this house, at a very low price, and he fears that the owner, driven out in 1948 and wanting to regain his property, might have sent the photographer to document the situation. Mihaï, for example, is a student of mathematics who lives with his parents in a very large apartment, close to Plaza Romana, right in the center of Bucharest. Five enormous rooms, piles and piles of books — for a rent of 1,000 lei, he tells us ($2 in 1992). Privatization and the return of uncontrolled rents will be a catastrophe.

Securitate and political considerations apart, how could any renter or owner not be distressed by the decline of a formerly splendid neighborhood? These patrician houses of dilapidated stucco, these private mansions with the graceful awnings, these miniature palaces crumbling into disrepair among their wisteria-shaded terraces, with broken-down cars rusting along the sidewalks, all this speaks of a tragedy without remedy, a collapse, a disaster so absolute that no restoration seems possible. The survivors wander about, adrift in their memories and their obsessions. Was the explosive gent on strada Silvestru terrified that he would be thrown out? Or were his fears more profound? Does he feel trapped like a blind bat in his dilapidated villa, knocking against the walls of an interminable nightmare? This mixture of aggressiveness, of rundown mansions, and perfect French culture speaks volumes about the conflicts that are devastating Romanian society.

These conflicts are masterfully depicted in a book by a young writer from Bucharest, whose novel takes place between strada Venerei and avenue Ştefan the Great (which can be reached by going up strada Galatzi to the north). It is commonly believed in France that all Romanian writers of any value live in Paris and write in French. It is also commonly believed that a dictatorship as harsh as that of Ceausescu must have choked off any creativity. The friends of Romania sadly believed that the country had no writer with the force of Jerzy Andrzejewski in Poland, of Bohumil Hrabal in Czechoslovakia. But *The Dream*, by Mircea Cartarescu, is the novel they were waiting for, the proof that intellectual and spiritual life, far from being vanquished in Romania, burns there with an intensity that is not very common in the West.

The book is not flawless, certainly, but overall it breathes with a vitality, an energy, and a rage that grip the reader.*

The Dream is above all a novel about Bucharest: Bucharest with its Stalinist concrete avenues, but also the maze of its curving lanes, secret gardens, abandoned mansions, ruined 1900's architecture, and even more so, about its labyrinth of neuroses, nightmares, and eccentricities.

The main character is an architect, Emil Popescu, who manages, through little deals and of draconian economies, to buy a car, which he parks in front of his building. While waiting to obtain a driving license, he visits the car, sits in the driver's seat, and plays with the gearshift, until the day when he discovers the virtues of the horn. The original horn that comes with a Dacia appears too modest to him; he gets his hands on a musical horn with six notes. One after another, he installs increasingly complicated apparatuses, on which he starts to improvise melodies. To such an extent that a Japanese who has heard of his prowess sends him an organ that can be connected to the battery. He scarcely leaves the car again; his wife deserts him; the wheels and engine are stolen; but he sits there, with his fingers growing ever longer, competing in celestial harmonies with the cosmos. This superb apologue hints at many of the distortions that warp daily life in Romania. Getting a car is so rare, so exceptional, that it already borders on the fantastic. Even without a driver's license, without gas or tires, one can always play the horn, until one is dizzy, until one is delirious.

His writing slips little by little into the grotesque and the absurd. In another scene, some tough boys and girls are playing in a construction site. They are joined by a delicate youngster whom one would think might become their victim; but no, through his subtle charm, enchanting story-telling and the bizarreness of the theories that he professes, he soon becomes their leader. He speaks as if he were in a dream. And that is the secret of transcendency that he embodies, and that is the general sense of the book: that Romanian reality has been so abused, so ridiculed for centuries, so emptied of substance and value, that the only real reality is to be sought in dreams.

Southern (or Oriental) Easygoing Charm versus the Force of Reason

Magheru Avenue was cut through the city after World War II. It seems to have been added in an effort to infuse a little rationality into the oriental labyrinth that was old Bucharest. As in any town where the houses were built first, and then streets were built around them, Bucharest shows that the boyars set up their residences before thinking of making any connection between them. Whimsy, chance, the desire to preserve the landscaping made this city an outpost of the Levant, an anarchistic jumble. From time to time, someone takes a brutal initiative to try to superimpose elements of harmony and efficiency. Ceausescu is criticized for deciding to widen or extend the principal traffic corridors (a problem that, in fact, every city eventually has to tackle). The legend has it that one morning he decided to "improve" one of the old roads; the police ordered the residents to move out, without notice. They couldn't decide what to take with them, so they ended up taking only the *cozonac,* the rich cakes they had prepared for Easter Sunday.

Paul Morand's book, *Bucharest,* is not only a masterpiece of travel writing, he makes it clear that Ceausescu did not invent this approach to Romanian city planning. To the south of the city, several public monuments crown the hill of Dealu Spirei: the Parliament, the church of the Patriarchy, the patriarch's palace. And here is what happened, in the pre-war years. The avenue that surges up the hill and gives access to these national institutions was laid out so decisively and carved out in such haste that the home-owners along its path were given no time to adapt to the declivity being dug through their yards; so that one beautiful morning they realized that their ground floor had become the second floor and their garages were accessible only to low-flying airplanes; their front doors opened onto thin air." Since 1935, therefore, the desire to "fix" what happened by chance and things taking their course, through sudden forceful action, has caused considerable shock. [*Ed. note*: In a similar vein, one can only imagine how shocked old Moscow must have been when the highway engineers took over; and shelves of books have been written to criticize the destruction that preceded Haussmann's proud avenues that are now among the pleasantest aspects of Paris.]

And even more recently, it seems to me that capitalist rapacity has caused far more damage in Western towns than Ceausescu caused by his efforts to modernize Romania. How much of the historic charm of France, Belgium, and Switzerland were destroyed in the 1960's to make

Bucharest: the old city (F.F.)

room for commercial buildings and shopping centers? Who protested when the 15th *arrondissement* in Paris was demolished? Or when the banks of the Seine were turned into highways? And wasn't the center of Brussels, today such a jarring mishmash, one of the most beautiful scenes of old Europe? Basle has been so disfigured by real estate speculation that it is hard to find any of the remaining lovely streets of old. These massacres do not justify the misdeeds of heavy-handed communist action; but they do deprive us of the right to point fingers. Is the dictatorship of money more virtuous than others?

While Ceausescu razed some villages, he was not the first, nor the most violent, in his destruction. In 1928, Panaït Istrati dedicated his book *The Thistles of Baragan* as follows:

I dedicate this book:
To the people of Romania,
to the eleven thousand assassinated
by the Romanian Government
at the three villages of Stanilesti, Baïlesti, and Hodivoïa,
felled by gunshot.
Crimes perpetrated in March 1907
and still unpunished.

Oriental fatalism and a Mediterranean easy-going nature are combined in the soul of Bucharest. There is something almost Arabic about this city, and something Neapolitan as well. It becomes clear that Romania is a country of the south, during the long autumn, when the thermometer in October still hits 85°. The summer heat — which slams abruptly into the vicious winter — is often unbearable. The combination of Levantine resignation and southern nonchalance gives the capital its charm. Only the political leaders, municipal officials and architects occasionally sense the danger that results from such a relaxed approach, and succumb to the urge to make a sudden swing toward modernity. Well before Communism, such reactions were seen.**

Calea Victoriei, an avenue that runs more or less parallel to Magheru, from north to south, avoids the straight-arrow approach and instead meanders like the mood of the first residents (it thus embodies license as Magheru embodies geometry), offering several testaments of this combat between the forces of reason and the southeastern pen-

Bucharest: Carul cu Bere restaurant

chant for disorder and ruin. This combat is always pathetic, it is so un-equal; even though the will to fight against Byzantium does not always go as far as creating the ghastly copy of Moscow, ugly, gray and frozen, represented by Magheru.

Calea Victoriei used to be called Podul Mogoshoaia, i.e. "bridge" or "floor." The road was built over the soft mud of the old marsh, on beams that supported cars and pedestrians after a fashion. It allowed the prince to go from his city palace to Mogoshoaia, his summer resi-dence, along the curvilinear route between the residences of his boyards. Where did they get this modern name of "Victory"? To what victory does it refer? What historical event has this people, who have been continuously occupied, despoiled, and humiliated by more power-

Bucharest: old city villas

ful neighbors, found to praise? The name was adopted after the battle of Plevna, in 1877, in a Bulgarian city where the Russians, with the critical help from the Romanian army, defeated the Turks. The Romanians were on the Russians' side: the defeat of the Divan, and their astute diplomacy used against the Russian threat, delivered them from their hereditary enemies. The substitution of the word "Victory," sonorous and bright, for the dull "Podul," which evoked heavy splashing and slips in the mud, illustrates the first effort toward rationality, the first act of confidence in the future, the first sense of conviction that it might be possible to overcome an obstinately contrary fate — although the avenue retained its archaic and sinuous form.

Heading north from Plaza Victoriei you can see, on the right, a staircase flanked by two lions, leading to an enormous glass canopy in the shape of a scallop shell, sheltering the entrance the old Cantacuzino palace. With its corbelled balconies and opulence worthy of Haussmann, it dates from the end of the 19th century, a golden age for Bucharest, following the establishment of the kingdom, made independent by the Congress of Berlin of 1878. Cantacuzino was among the highest aristocracy, along with Brancovan and Chika. The interior of the palace is even more eclectic than the façade: the oval atrium-salon, with a gallery encircling the second story and a naked woman painted on the ceiling, molded stucco and gilt ornamentation, it seems like a baroque candy box. There is no true baroque in Romania. All the rounded or ovoid constructions, all the flamboyant ornamentation that would appear to deserve the epithet of "baroque," date from the 1900's; they are a

mixture of Art Nouveau and kitsch, the Romanian adaptation of an outdated style, a wish to catch up with a missed era, the expression of inconsolable nostalgia. "In Romania, we like the Baroque," I was told by Dolores Toma, a specialist in this art, "because we feel that it connects us to Western Europe." There is a constant desire to get the better of the East, that has been generous only in plunderers and in torture, from the Turks and later from the Russians.

It was in this palace that George Enescu first played the principal movement of his opera *Œdipus*, on November 19, 1922, an opera that would have been granted a prominent place among the great masterpieces of the century, between *Pelléas* and *Wozzeck*, if it were not for the prejudice that diminished everything that comes from Romania. Indeed, the work was not included in the French edition of Kobbé until 1991!

Enescu, born to a peasant family in Bukovina but already elevated by a successful career that made the cottage in Liveni a distant memory, met Marouka Rosetti, wife of Cantacuzino, in 1910. Tall, slender, strong-featured as an icon, the queen of elegance in Bucharest, she lived in this palace illuminated by torches as though in the inner sanctum of a harem. After her husband died, Marouka, as passionate as she was beautiful, had been consumed by an unrequited passion. Spurned, in despair, she set herself on fire with gasoline. She was saved, but her face was terribly scarred; she would no longer show herself in public without a plaster mask. Enescu, with a peasant's fascination for princesses, asked her to marry him. He was 58 when they wed, on December 4, 1939, and so he moved into the palace. Every morning, from her bed, through a notch in the closed draperies behind which she hid her ravaged features, Marouka would waggle a finger to greet the violonist, who would be waiting to help her with her plaster. When they had guests, they would leave the salons dark with shadows. One antique lamp gave out a faint gleam, and guests had to feel their way between the furniture to greet the mistress of the house, where she would recline on a divan draped in red velvet.

Her great rival in Bucharest, in the 1910's, was none other than Helene Chrisoveleni, princess Soutzo by marriage, who later became the wife of Paul Morand. She was born in Galati, on the Danube, just a few miles from Braïla (but light years away from Panaït Istrati, socially). Greek through her father and Triestine by her mother, she was a member of that clan of mysterious beauties (including Anna de Noailles and Marthe Bibescu) who made Romanian beauties the rage in Paris after the war. She was very petite but very proud of carriage, her head always held very high; Cocteau called her a "Minerva who swallowed her owl." Proust fell in love with her during a dinner party; he left in the middle of the night to wake up the musicians of the Poulet Quartet and have them serenade the princess with a quartet by Caesar Franck. This happened at the Ritz Hotel, where she lived, as the daughter and sister of bankers who controlled the finances of Balkans as well as part of the oil extracted from Romanian lands.

A little further along the avenue, you can turn left by Biserica Amzei (a church) and find a lively market, across the street from the French embassy. Despite the periodic food shortages, it is colorful and picturesque. Peasant women bring the produce from their gardens. Old women stand behind their rudimentary folding tables and sell their peppers (red, yellow or green, stacked in pyramids, crisp and fresh, the *ardei iute*, as refreshing as cool water and a perfect counterbalance to the rich pork dishes of Romanian cuisine), tomatoes, carrots, turnips and all kinds of unfamiliar root vegetables. Here and there, a solitary egg might be displayed, on its own, like a miracle. Part of the market is covered with a canopy; flowers are sold there, and wooden kitchen implements, handmade brooms, baskets and Turkish slippers, rustic but comfortable. None of the vendors says anything, everyone seems quite indifferent; is this simple resignation, given the poverty of the goods, or is it the weak purchasing power of the customers that discourages any special sales effort?

Going back to Calea Victoriei, you can see, down on the left, the Athenaem, an imposing rotunda preceded by a neo-classical peristyle. This building was designed in the late 1880's, and its façade demonstrates a touching desire to project the "nobility" of straight and regular lines; but at the same time, since this parody of ancient Greece is a little out of place here, it embodies the difficulties of any such attempt. The interior decor contradicts the efforts of the exterior: the ceiling, in deep red stucco, transforms the pseudo-Hellenistic Pantheon into a campy dancehall. Concerts are held here — George Enescu directed Beethoven's *Ninth Symphony* in 1914, its Romanian debut. (Some people will be appalled at this cultural backwardness, and others will wonder

whether the richness of Romania's traditional music, the poignant beauty of the melancholic *doïna*, the magical spells of the panpipes, are not legitimate grounds for a certain indifference to the erudite creations of the West.)

The traditional Enescu contest was held here in September 1991, after an interruption of more than twenty years. Mady Mesplé, a judge in the vocal contest, said she was impressed by the quality of the competitors but regretted the lack of publicity and the sparse foreign participation. The Romanian school has produced sopranos of worldwide renown, such as Evghenia Moldoveanu, Mariana Nicolescu and, more recently, Leontina Vaduva and Angela Gheorghiu (both of whom sang lead roles at Lincoln Center, New York, in spring of 2000).

The Bucharest Opera, however, remains mired in outdated conventions. We saw part of *La Traviata*: it was the second act, since here you can walk in at any time during the show and take a seat at random, as though it were a caravanserai open to wayfaring travelers. The director of a French ballet company, who was touring with his troupe, acknowledged his discouragement. He had wanted to lower a spotlight on a boom, and was informed that the equipment had not been used in fifty years, and would fall apart on contact. The actors are in the habit of positioning themselves only in the center of the stage, facing directly outward, with the light shining directly on their faces; the drama of indirect lighting, so much preferred by French performers, seems not to be used, here. This tale seems to me to summarize old-fashioned logic (frontal lighting, static positioning); this combines with the dilapidation of the equipment to make the Bucharest Opera a mausoleum for Romanian disappointments.

The Athenaeum Palace, a deluxe hotel and the most beautiful in Bucharest from the 1930's, was vacant for many years; [*Editor's note*: In the mid-1990's it was taken over by Hilton and has been recreated as a posh international business hotel]. The old royal palace, which borders the Plaza Gheorgiu-Dej, is in full splendor although its heavy neoclassical façade (a style that is not entirely compatible with the Romanian vivacity), was damaged during the revolution (or the "so-called revolution") of 1989. What is most regretful is the damage done to several paintings that were housed there in the Museum of Fine Art. The

Bucharest: Athenaeum Româm

Central University Library, opposite the palace, was devastated by fire during the upheavals of 1989 and remained a charred ruin for some years.[†] This was a twofold tragedy for the Romanians, such avid readers: the loss of so many books, and a spectacular defeat of Reason. The old Communist Party headquarters, white and symmetrical, is still intact with all its doctrinal frigidity. Ceausescu apostrophized his people for the last time from this balcony, before escaping in a helicopter that was waiting on the roof.

Back on Calea Victoriei, here, on the left, is the little Cretsulescu church, erected in 1722. There are hardly any older churches in Bucharest; they all are rather pretty, but not noteworthy, brick cakes cut from the same mold, with double cupolas and, inside, the smoky obscurity of the orthodox rite. In a covered gallery nearby there is a second-hand book shop, with a limited selection, and here too is Bucharest's main record store (which doesn't say much, for they have only about fifty titles). The records, like the books, will not be re-issued when the stock runs out. I hurried to buy some of Enescu's works.

Capşa

Further down on the left, we come to Edgar-Quinet street, named for one of the first in France to express sympathy towards Romania by calling it "our Latin sister." This historian's democratic convictions and virulent anticlericalism had quite an influence on the young nation. They should have listened to him more closely! More than a century ago, he observed that, "Russia's friendship was more disastrous to Romania than the hostility of all the other nations together."

In Paris, Edgar-Quinet boulevard runs past a cemetery — so this adversary of Napoleon III has been condemned to a second death. But here in Bucharest, Edgar Quinet is the guarantee not only of life, but of wellbeing and gluttony. Where his street intersects Calea Victoriei, the house on the corner is the site of the legendary Capsha, which used to be the most famous restaurant in the capital and can still offer a good meal. Capsha, a young Bucharestian, was apprentice confectioner at Le Boissier in Paris, in the mid-1800's. He joined the Muscovite general staff during the Russo-Turkish war, and was ruined by cossacks who plundered his carriages full of caramels, barley sugar and pralines.

With all the sweetness gone out of his life, he made his way back, on foot, to Bulgaria, where he had the happy idea of teaching the Bulgarians to make rose-petal jam. Having become rich once again, he came back to Bucharest, and opened up a hotel, restaurant, confectionery and coffee shop, which became a favorite with the upper crust of Bucharest society. Little remains, now, except the private dining rooms in the restaurant, which still exhibited a "sublime classicism, " as Morand says, with its velvet, ebony furniture and frosted mirrors. The prices are so high that only tourists come here.

It is hard to find good food in Bucharest, these days. In fact, it is hard to find any decent meal on the street, given the shortage of restaurants and the unreliable supplies. Since Capsha is so well-known, you need a reservation (or better yet, an introduction by an influential friend). The menu is not very extensive but for Romania it is fairly good. Avoid anything called "cordon bleu" or "filet mignon." The Romanians have a passion for meat, but the cattle population is not cooperative. The typical (recommended) menu starts with a plate of hot meat hors d'oeuvres: liver pâtés, lamb rolls, meatballs and croquettes. Or you might try a *ciorba*, an excellent sour soup featuring cabbage, potatoes and chicken or other meat. *Sarmale* are a good main dish (ground pork or lamb, wrapped in cabbage and simmered in broth, smothered in sour cream and topped with tomatoes), more interesting than the usual pork. The ritual accompaniment is composed of a salad of crudités (tomatoes, onions, sweet peppers, cucumbers) topped with *cascaval* cheese. To finish, the waiter offers a choice between coffee (very acceptable, Turkish, bracing) and sherbet.

Private restaurants began to appear in the mid-1990's. The young founders of Babel Publishing, Radu Toma and his wife Dolores, invite us to Velvet, the fashionable place in 1991 (it is rumored to have been financed by the wife of Prime Minister Petru Roman). The decor is brand new, pretentious, and screaming yellow. The seats are too low, and you can hardly get your knees under the table. In contradiction to the desire to be "modern," this seems like a surprising regression to the Turkish fashion — although that would be on soft cushions. The entire place is suffused with an impossible synthesis. The maitre d', stiff and serious as an undertaker's assistant, is affronted by my question about Romanian cuisine. "We strive to emulate Paris," he informs me. That seems to go for the prices, too. I calculate that the dinner will cost 600 lei ($3), almost a tenth of the basic wage. The grave-digger proposes "chateaubriants" and the inevitable "cordon bleu," but we choose the more traditional and less adventurous pig. Another scornful pout, and a categorical refusal when I tell him to bring me some of my dear *ardei*. They offer a strange list of desserts, from "Madamme Plaisir" to "Joffre" and "Joffre torta." "Madamme Plaisir" is tempting, with its double *m* that seems to herald some dense confection. However, they are out of "Plaisir" today. So we try the others. They are ridiculously miniscule and devoid of interest.

Privatization and the incipient market economy have caused harm far greater than these culinary stupidities, and the wind that blows from the West is causing negative effects in all fields. Our editor friend — an instructor at the University, like his wife — set up their own publishing house, out of a passion for literature. They begin to tell us about the difficulties of the trade. Paper prices are sky-high, printing equipment is expensive, the distribution system is in ruins, and Romania, like all the other former communist countries, has experienced a breakdown of the cultural apparatus that, although it was held in check by political and moral censorship, was however no shame to the regime. A book cost 15 *lei*, and people could read a lot. Today a book is 50 *lei*, and people read far less. (This can also be attributed to the proliferation of newspapers, over 1000 dailies! and the intoxication of freedom that has absorbed peoples purchasing power, exhausted their appetite for reading, and eaten up the paper resources. The average Romanian seems to go through three or four newspapers per day. Nevertheless, Radu prints 30,000 copies of each of the 5 books that he publishes per year (the lack of paper prevents him from printing more), and thesea are foreign authors perfectly unknown in Romania — a print run that Western editors only dream of. "I expect to sell them within the month," he adds. "If not, it would be a disaster." His compatriots' intellectual appetite combined with the scarcity of titles and the relevance of Radu's selections make a success here of an enterprise that would surely fail in Paris.

On our first visit, in 1990, Radu and Dolores had hosted us in their apartment and treated us to a succulent meal, in the great Romanian tradition. At that time there was almost nothing in the shops, and in any case the lines were interminable — and consistsed mostly of retirees, of old people. How our hosts managed? "Oh!" they answered, "We

are fortunate to have parents who are still in good shape." That expresses the nobility with which the Romanians adapt to the pathos of
daily life. Today, with the partial liberalization of prices, shortages are
less acute but many normal goods are beyond the reach of most people.

After Gheorghiu-Dej Boulevard, on the left, we come to the little

Bucharest: Hanul Manuc

church where the hand of Saint Cyprian is preserved (a black hand, shrunken, a monkey's claw fixed on an ebony arm) then Stavropoleos Street, where it is worth the trouble to enter the homonymous church, one of prettiest in Bucharest, and especially the Carul Cu Bere, "The Beer Keg," a famous literary café in gothic-kitsch style. This is like Faust's tavern transposed into opera-like décor, with gilded arches, carved wooden balconies, spiral staircases, historical scenes painted on the walls, and colored canopies. For lack of light bulbs, the atmosphere is dark and not very merry. What's more, we couldn't get a beer: the waiter could only offer mineral water and a carbonated beverage with orange, dreadful, a purgative that would drive away Mephisto.

Still in search of a beer, we went further along past the church and took Covaci Street, stopping in at another church, Curtea Veche, "the Old Heart." Here we go into the oldest and the largest hostelry in Bucharest: an enormous courtyard (big enough to accommodate a caravan), bordered by beautiful arcades supporting carved wooden galleries, and tables full of customers. Strapping young lasses deliver gargantuan glasses of beer covered with foam, which they bring in their large bare arms ten or twelve at the same time, like in a Hofbraühaus of Munich. However, the atmosphere, in spite of this excess of the flesh and tankards, is in no way Bavarian, and one would hesitate to call such a poetic place a brewery. It is still called Hanul Manuc (Manuc Inn), named for Manuc Bey who built it early in the 1800's as a caravanserai. I noted a heap of straw in the middle of the courtyard, and a hen house in the corner. Only horses and uncoupled wagons are missing, now. When Morand was here, he still saw campfires and carts. This is the meeting place, the legendary inn from oriental tales, where one could expect to meet travelers coming from Trebizond, Burgas or Odessa; Hanul Manuc is not a tower but a court of Babel, and exemplifies Bucharest's cosmopolitan past.

In 1995, the most fashionable restaurant was the Transylvania. Opened in 1993, it serves the well-to-do, charging $30 a meal (half a month's wages!). The cuisine is excellent. Their policy is more sensible than some of the other places we've mentioned: you can get the Romanian traditional dishes, such as *mititei* and *kiftele* (lamb and pork meatballs), *sarmale*, and a rich *mamaliga*. The decor is quintessentially nouveau riche. On the ground floor, the salons are upholstered in red velvet, with white walls with gilded mouldings, ornate armchairs, with

gilded backs. Downstairs we visited the Italian salon (carved oak furniture), the Viennese salon (for only two guests, as rococo as possible),
the German salon (decidedly rustic), the Dracula salon (intricate
woodwork, two rooms connected by a very low arched passageway, a
kind of self-conscious medieval replica). It's all high kitsch, and must
reflect the tastes of the new Mafia. The self-importance of the red salons is reminiscent of the Ceausescu palace.

We went there on a Saturday evening. We were made to wait a
few minutes in an anteroom, also red, although the restaurant was
empty. A bit of ceremony, before sitting down! The tablecloths are
damask, the plates are hand-painted, the napkins are presented on a
silver tray. Young men in red jackets present the menus, but it is a
young lady who served us. A beautiful face and very nice figure, a little
skirt gathered by a knot at the back. She delivered and cleared away
the dishes without raising her eyes, like an idol that allows one to con-
template, to desire, without returning one's glances. When she was
leaving our table she would back away, and turn around only when she
was a few paces away from the guests. A compliment on the quality of
the food won a wan smile, quickly suppressed. Is this impassible mien
ordered by the management? Is it that she fears the coarse behavior
that the new nabobs might allow themselves? Or a piquant touch,
added knowingly to her natural grace? Romanian women are no sav-
ages, and perhaps the customers, if they spend so much money at Transylvania, are happy to find some mystery there.

The Château

Finally, at the very end of Calea Victoriei, is a neighborhood that
has cropped up just in the 1990's and that is not mentioned on any
maps despite the fact that it covers hundreds of acres. Is it that there
wasn't enough paper to record this astonishing innovation, or did the
inhabitants think that by refusing to acknowledge it with an official act
of identification, they can deny what they consider an object of shame
and horror?

An avenue as wide as the Champs-Élysée and several miles long,
lined by imposing, expensive-looking white buildings, better-built than
the dull gray houses on Magheru, leads to the main façade of the gigan-

Bucharest: Ceauşescu Palace

tic palace that Ceausescu had built in 1983, on the site of a neighborhood the size of a small arrondissement in Paris. The revolution broke out before the palace was finished; the main work, however, was completed. Seeing this powerful, austere, cold construction at the end of

the gigantic avenue, isolated on a vast, vacant site, this enormous marble mass (pardon all the adjectives), with a symmetrical interplay of columns and arcades that recalls simultaneously a fortress, a temple and a mausoleum, it seems to me that with this monument Ceausescu wanted to ensure the final victory of rationality over chaos, to affirm creative dynamism and modernistic élan, but that it could hardly have been turned out more ironically. What could be more misguided than to cut off the natural growth of a city, destroying in order to rebuild; what could be more bizarre and out of context than this effort toward reason?

Not that the façade is ugly; in fact, I rather like it. My Romanian friends think I am lying, or teasing, when I say that. They don't want to think about this last, ruinous whim, of their president. They probably never noticed how the high round pilasters, linking the four stories in one upward movement, give the building an unexpected lightness. It was Bernin who first thought of minimizing the visual divisions between the horizontal levels, by using pilasters that cover the entire height of the building, providing a sweeping vertical line that tricks the eye with the illusion of vertical energy. They have also not noticed that the overall layout, a square extended by four star-shaped pavilions, reflects (on a gigantic scale that somehow distorts the overall effect) the invention of another Italian baroque architect, Juvara, at the château of Stupinigi, near Turin. We should also note that the façade, rather than appearing static and flat, has been artfully designed with setbacks and an alternation of right angles and horseshoe arcades, so that it gives a lively, dynamic feeling.

As an exceptional favor, we were allowed to visit the interior, which is closed to public since no one has come up with a use for it. The architect who guided us, flanked by an officer, provided certain statistics; he seemed half-impressed, half-depressed by the enormity of the figures involved. They call this the "Palace of the People," but I prefer to call it "the Château." With its threatening monumentality, its mysterious omnipresence, and the obsession that it exudes (all the more weird since nobody has the right to visit it), it embodies Kafka's malevolent Utopia. I notice that we kept our voices low while we were there, and avoided making too much noise with our footsteps. It is 210 feet high, and covers 900 acres. The height was originally supposed to be 150 feet. Ceausescu himself — he came to inspect it every weekend — altered the model and expanded the dimensions. The overall project manager was a woman, Anka Petrescu, with a team of 200 architects, 300 engineers and 20,000 workmen. Twenty billion *lei* was spent so far; it would take another 5 billion to finish the job. (I can't help thinking — although I wouldn't mention this sacrilegious thought to our hosts — that someday the Château will become a tourist attraction and money-maker, and they will forget what it cost, the way we've forgotten the millions wasted on Versailles, the way we've forgotten that hundreds of Swiss workmen, who dug the canals and reflecting pools in the park, died of malaria.)

We entered through the southern façade, to the left of the main façade. There is no furniture, but the walls, the floors, and the staircase are in place. Everything is marble, and the scintillating polish makes the rooms, the endless galleries, seem even emptier. This useless disproportion has a magical fascination: furnished, the spaces will lose much of their appeal. For the moment, there is nothing but chandeliers. Ceausescu had an obsession for chandeliers; big chandeliers, with crystal pendants gleaming under hundreds of bulbs, all lit. This detail struck me as particularly incongruous given that, the day of our visit, the shortage of light bulbs was such that our room in the Bucharest (one of most luxurious hotels in the capital) had only a 25-watt light, and it took much diplomacy and another pack of Marlboros to get anything better.

The main staircase, which splits into two banks of stairs, in the baroque style, leads us to one of Ceausescu's offices. It's sixty feet by thirty, with three lofty windows and three monumental chandeliers. Neo-classic woodwork floor-to-ceiling, with grooved pilasters and intricate capitals. Heavy curtains of embroidered damask. An immense carpet. Given the majesty of the proportions and the meticulous craftsmanship, the décor is neither ridiculous nor heavy. The desk had been placed at one end, so that the visitor would have to traverse twenty meters under the gaze of the prince: an old trick of rulers everywhere. Ceausescu would have used this office in his capacity as Secretary of the Communist Party; he had two others, one for the President of the Republic and one for the chief of the armed forces. The office of the Party Secretary communicates with a waiting room, with lighter woodworks, five (smaller) chandeliers, hand-woven Gobelin tapestries, and a French carpet. The salon opens on the other side to Mrs. Ceausescu's office: the proportions are a little less immodest, with only one chandelier, and the woodwork and furniture (already installed) are Louis XV. Louis XIV for the great leader, Louis XV for his wife: nuances that subtly differentiate male power and female power, and show how the president was able to emulate the example of the French monarchy.

The southern façade was reserved for the Party, the western façade (not finished) for the banquet halls, the northern façade for the Parliament. The State, the Government used the eastern entrance, the main façade. This distribution of functions according to the points of the compass can be read as symbolic. The West, generally disdained, was allotted to banquets and empty ceremonies. The Party turned toward the sun, the Parliament was exposed to the cold — an indication of the hierarchy of the political entities. East is for the State: Ceausescu uncoupled his country from the Soviet train in vain (although at first, this earned him considerable popularity in the West, including state visits from presidents de Gaulle and Nixon, which for a long time sealed his international reputation); but Asia continued to fascinate Ceausescu. In spite of the marble, the rigor, and the severity of the Château, putting his office as Head of State on the east side seems to undermine his intention of extirpating the influence of the East. This office is even grander than that of the Party Secretary: seventy feet by seventy, the State as a regular square. More woodwork, and no fewer than twelve chandeliers. The terrorism of rationality always aims for geometrical perfection: think of Robespierre, with his calculated gestures, his cold demeanor, the feigned languor that he affect as the supreme leader, the triumphal arches drawn up on the esplanades, the trees planted in too-straight a line, like an abstract flame of his spirit.

On two stories, on the east, extends the Hall of Romania: 200 feet long, 100 feet wide, 80 feet high, with eleven windows opening onto the circular plaza where the gigantic avenue begins.[††] The carpet alone weighs three tons. The architect accompanying us opens the central window, and we go out on the balcony, the tribune from which the president had harangued the crowds gathered below. If the interior of the Château, with all its pomp and formal whiteness, its surrealist emptiness, evokes the Rome of Mussolini, this balcony, these columns, the plaza, the avenue lined with white buildings, all these touches that were intended to lend more weight to the word of the Chief take us further back in time, to the basilica of Saint-Peter itself. The majestic sanctuary seems to superimpose itself on the Château — the persistent nostalgia for Urbs. Emperor Trajan, in antiquity, conquered what was then called Dacia. Today's Romania still hearkens back to old Dacia and its contact with the Roman legions. In his fight against Byzantine influences, Ceausescu turned to Rome — while secularizing the model. Above the balcony, the architect draws our attention to a marble cross inscribed in the entry staircase: purely decorative, he affirms, but every time Ceausescu was visiting they hid this ornament, which he would have seen as a Christian symbol.

Accompanying us back through the rooms and the galleries, our guide mentioned that the palace will need some modifications if it is to be used for day-to-day business. It takes too long to get from one space to another; there are too few staircases and elevators. Too few bathrooms, too — it is all more symbolic than functional.

On January 1, 1935, Paul Morand attended the blessing of the Royal Palace that had been just completed. He described the luxury, the ostentation of the interior, "galleries of arms and armor, arcades, rotundas and porticos, all the high elements of classical architecture," and crowds of dignitaries strangled in their formal dress. Sixty years

Bucharest: Lipscani street today

later, one can imagine that this description would have been apt during the dedication of this palace, as well.

As of 1995, the Parliament took occupancy of the palace, as a symbol of democracy. And some of the chambers are used for concerts, exhibitions, and fashion shows, symbols of the nation's rebirth.

Gypsies

Mrs. X, a Romanian living in Paris and visiting Bucharest for the first time in 23 years, looks at the Château with mixed feelings. She cannot prevent herself from seeing the appeal of the grand edifice, much as she despises its author. I thought I would mention, so that she didn't think I was minimizing the errors of the dictator, that he tore down an entire district to fulfill this whim. To my great surprise, she pursed her mouth and said, "Oh! it was only a Gypsy camp; no one came here, there was nothing but shacks, and dusty lanes full of pigs and chickens." The Romanians hated Ceausescu, but they detest the Gypsies even more. To such a degree that this old Bucharestian let herself confuse her memories. There were precious few Gypsies in these parts; it was a petit-bourgeois area, with 19th century houses, perhaps lacking in character but in no way disreputable. "No historic value," other friends assured me — with a hint of disappointment, as though they would have liked to be able to blame Ceausescu for more — "but with a bit of charm." I often heard, as we would pass a Gypsy on the street, "In Ceausescu's day, they had disappeared. We never saw them. And now they are back, in force."

What is the basis of such racism? The Romanian relates to the Gypsy as the Pole does to the Jew, the American to the Black, and the Frenchman to the Arab: they fear "the other," the one who is different, and moreover poorer, hungrier, and therefore more dangerous to the community. Romanians seem to me to be far less anti-Semitic than the Poles, because the Gypsy is the lightning rod for all their xenophobia. "They are called also 'Romany,' and for good reason. They are a Romanian national problem, which you cannot understand." Ah, the distortions of mistrust! That is a false etymology. "Romany" has nothing to do with "Romania," it comes from the Gypsies' own word for their people, "roma," since "rom" means "man."

Previous page: Neagoie Basarab, Prince of Vallachia (1512-1521)

According to Paul Labbé, anti-Semitism was virulent in 1913. In Iashi, Moldova, the author visited "a low district, incredibly dirty and foul-smelling, crawling with vermin and children. This is where the real masters of the city live: the Jews. The Romanians scorn them, but they have been conquered by them; the Jews hold them in their hands. With tireless patience, with unrivaled skill, they have little by little gained a monopoly over all trade, and they have ruined the peasants; everyone owes them money. They are insatiable; they have money, and they want more. They are the leeches of Romania." One of Labbé's guides told him, "Even with their eyes closed, a Romanian can recognize, by smell, whether a village is populated with Jews." In Moldova and Wallachia (i.e. Romania before the First World War), there were six hundred synagogues.

What Labbé heard as far as the Gypsies was quite another story. "Look how handsome they are!" someone said to him. Whereas the Jews disgusted him, with their unwashed hair in "corkscrews," their "small eyes," their "red eyelids," their "curved spines," the Romanian was filled with wonder at the Gypsy physique. "Slender and tanned, they are superb men; lascivious and dignified, even though dressed in rags, the women dance. . ." Of course, they are robbers, but so what; their wives are so attractive! "They are the sons of Love and Freedom," my Serb friends say. They have the air of a very ancient nobility, which explains their grand airs."

The genocide having put a brake on anti-Semitism, the Gypsies remain the sole object of denigration and hatred. Even aesthetic admiration, it seems to me, is only grudgingly admitted. However, among all the kinds of racism, this example does offer some extenuating circumstances. The Gypsies themselves refuse to assimilate. They resist moving into houses, they live along the roadside and deliberately keep to the margins of society. Moreover, in the background is the Romanian desire to reject anything that smacks of eastern influence. Rumored to have come from India, originally, the Gypsies, by their nomadism, their rejection of law, their refusal to be integrated into the nation that accommodates them, and the features of an ancient ethnic group are inherently incompatible with a modern State. No one knows how many of them there are in Romania, since they do not register their marriages. Thus, it is quite natural that the Romanians, in their effort toward order, rationality, and efficiency, seek to separate themselves from a law-

⟨ 173 ⟩

less people that only serve to emphasize their own lackadaisical tendencies, their Levantine atavism. The same person who told me that the baroque style is popular in Romania because they feel it connects them to Western Europe, added: "If we do not love the Gypsies, it is because they connect us to the East, to the Balkans;" in other words, to that turbid and tempting world that is still fascinating.

For the French, who sometimes feel stifled by Colbert's imposition of the worship of reason, utility, and productivity, it is easy to find the Gyspies amusing or attractive. Elsewhere, the presence of a race that is obstinately rebellious to the discipline of the State has a different effect. It is true that some of my fondest memories are related to meetings with the Gypsies. Even in Bucharest, we crossed their world twice: in its popular form in Lipscani Street, and in its more refined form during a wedding at the Hotel Bulevard.

Strada Lipscani crosses Calea Victoriei and connects with the extension of Magheru. The name *Lipscani* goes back to the remote time when the merchants of Leipzig came to sell their fabrics. The narrow and sinuous street is still the site of commerce and minor trading in everyday goods. One of the causes of the Romanians' animosity toward this tribe would be their own lack of business acumen. The Romanians have always relied on others to look after their practical interests; they let the Frenchmen build their monuments (such as the Athenaeum, the Savings Bank, the State Bank), the Germans their railroads, the Englishmen their sewers; and they left the Jews and the Gypsies to buy and resell the articles necessary for everyday life. In recent times of shortage, the role of these intermediaries has become more important. The Gypsies occupy Strada Lipscani, and when I say "occupy," I mean they don't just fill the shops but spill out into the sidewalk and the street with their tables and wares.

You can scarcely make your way through the crowd. A tiny transistor radio, on the ground, lets out some Arab music and the young people gather around it. A street pedlar pulls a series of incredible trinkets out of his sack, and a cluster of customers gathers around him. Old clothes blow in the wind, hanging on a display rod. The atmosphere reminded me of a souk in Tunis, of a Neapolitan *vicolo*. It is the revenge of the East on every attempt at occidentalization, it is the rout of the middle-class mercenary attitude, the triumph of illegality and anarchy. My Romanian friends are offended that I like something that they consider a cesspool, a scene of vice. "Come on, they are all robbers." Well, yes, business on this street has as much to do with sleight-of-hand and short-changing as with regular exchanges of goods for money; but how can I explain how refreshing it is to envelope oneself in the risky atmosphere where you take your chances, after the boredom of normal shops protected by doors and vitrines, and the reliable honesty of all parties?

We came across the Gypsy wedding several times as we went back and forth through the town that night. In the Hotel Bulevard, a troupe of Gypsies (apparently better-off than their cousins along the highway) were enjoying a sumptuous feast, and all evening long the bride, who in no way evoked any sense of virginity and whose anatomy was barely covered by her gown, undulated to the music for every eye to see. This sensual display, so much at odds with Christian (or Marxist) ideas of purity, is another indication of the basis for the Romanians' distaste for a primitive, albeit vital and sparkling, race.

Workshops, writers

We decide to visit few artists' studios. Several of them are clustered near the Television headquarters. Each little house is surrounded by a garden, which is used as a storage space and a dump. Constantin Lucaci receives us amidst his sculptures: stainless steel objects, polished, luminous, shaped like waves, spirals, rockets. He is about seventy years old, a VIP, author of monumental fountains in Bucharest, Constantza, Victoria. He exhibits regularly. The palace of Diamonds, in Ferrare, Italy, organized a retrospective of his works in 1982. Squat and round-faced, gruff, stubborn, and voluble, he comments on each piece without leaving us one moment of respite. Like many Romanians, he is anxious to justify himself. He harps on the "spiritual dimension" of this cold and brilliant world. The relations of volume and space, the dynamics of the curved lines alternating with sharp edges, the use of clear surfaces as mirrors that reflect the surrounding objects, he points out to us in turn each stage in the development of his "thinking." Nothing would be more unpleasant for him, apparently, than to allow us to believe that he works in abstraction. His meteorites all have a soul, and must invite the viewer to dialogue with the infinite. He wants to convince us of that, at all costs. Fifty years of Communism could explain this need to justify art by a greater social mission; but well before Communism, Brancusi, whose aerodynamic forms seem to have inspired our host, subordinated aesthetic concerns to a philosophical and moral idea. This seems to be a constant among Romanian artists, this quest for something greater.

Across from Constantin Lucaci, on the other side of the court, Georgeta Naparus camps out in a jumble of colors. She is a woman painter, with a heavy and powerful physique, and close-cropped grey hair; she's quiet, and lets us look at her canvases without trying to influence our judgment. Her paintings are drawn from popular imagery. Lines of figurines, posed flat on a red or orange background, look like pieces of an iconostasis: the same juxtaposition of small squares, the same meticulous accumulation, the same fear of empty space. Fresh and naive invention, strength and cheerfulness, and sometimes a touch of gold. It's an alliance of anecdotic and the timeless, a desire to draw parallels between folklore and myth.

However, "the most spiritual" of the Romanian artists whom we met was Sorin Dumitrescu, who is also a contributor to a religious magazine. Scorning the government-provided studios, he managed to get himself a place in an old villa, as dilapidated as it is poetic, and still showing vestiges of the splendors of the 1900's, in the main foyer. The other rooms are white and empty. He settles us in one of these rooms, against a wall, and then goes to look for one of the paintings that he wants to show us. He stands it on the ground, opposite us, against the white wall. It is a very elongated painting, like Holbein's *The Dead Christ*, in Basle, and this one, too, depicts a corpse. "A relic!" he exclaims. And he launches into an impassioned apology for all the religious relics, of which Romania, according to him, has a considerable stock, bought from the Greeks and the Turks.

He is big, powerful, bearded, and red; he has a child-like face, lost in priestly beard; he talks nonstop and presents his works with the consummate skill of a movie producer. When we are finished looking at one picture, he removes it to an adjoining room, then takes his time bringing in the next, meanwhile urging us to enjoy the wine that he has set before us. Apparently, it will help us attain the proper frame of mind for appreciating the unearthly qualities of his work.

The Wedding in Cana , painted late 1400s (Voroneţ)

Here, now, four Angels are aligned in front of us: four paintings, each one showing the same Angel, painted in greater and greater detail. They are large paintings, glorious in their androgyny, as he anxious to emphasize. Dumitrescu feels that androgyny is the seal of God. He took a traditional icon as a starting point, and rather than replicating the image, set out to create an exegesis, emphatic and merry, of the other-worldliness ignored by early icon painters. The chin of the Angel is prominent: a sign of masculinity, he insists; but at the same time, there is a relaxedness: a sign of the feminine. And the nose: effeminate, although sharp as a saber. And so on. He also shows us a series of angel's hands, as complexly symbolic as the faces. The work is splendid, at the same time lyrical and meticulous. Before we take our leave, we promise him that we will visit all the church relics that he enumerates for us, including the monkey hand of Saint Cyprian. "Go ahead, it is our speciality." He walks us back us to the street corner, then returns to his palace of dreams.

Sorin Dumitrescu is a legendary figure in Bucharest: for the exceptional quality of his art, for his vitality, and his persona as an enlightened painter who embodies the pantheist monk and the ribald peasant. The Art School students who accompanied us in our visits watched him in fascination. However, Dumitrescu is also criticized for his political positions. He is a friend of Father Justin; is no less reactionary than him, I am told, and no less unpleasant a fanatic.

The Romanian writers whom we met seemed to me to be paler, by contrast. Pen and paper do not provide the same gratification as a pot of painting, glazed clay and wood. Moreover, words are dangerous: under various regimes, the boldest have been locked up, and it's not clear that this practice can't be revived.

We went to visit several editorial offices. Every time we found the same thing: a huge reception room on the first floor of a 1900's mansion that had been converted into a "House of Writers"; and the same reception: the director and his assistants, lined up according to rank, who laid out before us every issue of their magazine (on poor, yellowy paper), while a Secretary carried in a tray with coffee. The magazines themselves testify pathetically to the superhuman combat required to provide a monthly forum for new literary talents. I realize that in Romania, a country of folk and oral tradition, poetry is more widespread and significant than the novel; and that short stories are also considered significant; and the principal function of these reviews, whose director and staff are generally poets themselves, is to publish short texts in verse or in prose. Everyone asked me how poetry is doing in France. And every time, not wishing to upset them too much with a brutal answer, I moderated my verdict and left some ray of hope shining.

How could I not recall Paul Celan, whose first poems appeared in 1945, in the Bucharest review *Agora*? One of the greatest 20th century poets in the German language, was born in Czernowitz (Cerneuț), in Bukovina. In 1941, the Germans deported his parents; in 1944, the Russians annexed his birthplace and the surrounding territory. He went to Bucharest, where he made his literary beginnings, and then moved onto Vienna and thence to Paris. His *La Fugue de la mort*, the title of one of his earliest and best-known pieces, could be seen as an emblem of all his work. A fugue, escape and death: taking refuge in Paris since 1948, he could never overcome his double misfortune as a Jew and a stateless person. One evening in April 1970, he put an end to his days by throwing himself into the Seine.

His friend from youth, Petru Solomon, emphasized the importance of his Romanian roots, in *Paul Celan, the Adolescence of a Good-bye* (Climats, Paris, 1990), despite the poet's choice of expressing himself in another language. One wonders very much why he chose German; some exegetes, considering the labor of disarticulation operated on the language of Goethe and Rilke, speculate that he was trying to kill the torturers who had killed his parents. In the twenty-odd years he spent in Paris, he did not write a single verse in French, although he had perfectly mastered the language. His Romanian poems, which date back to his three-year stay in Bucharest, were also worthy of attention, according to Petru Solomon. His *Love Song*, in spite of the title, actually shows that at the age of twenty-five the poet, obsessed with the idea of a "shipwreck" and "drowning," had already given up any hope of happiness.

At an amicable meeting at the "Museum of Literature," I was asked why, in France after the war, the writers tended to be leftist. "Which writers?" Aragon, Sartre. I explain to them that Aragon was an opportunist dandy, and Sartre a middle-class man who had a bad conscience over not being a working man. They shake their heads, disconcerted. For there is no Romanian word for "bad conscience." It translates as "guilt." At least that is unambiguous, and prevents any evasion into subtleties and the complex nuances of emotions.

Frederic takes us along to lunch with the princess Coco B. She is over 80 years old and lives in a two-room apartment in a concrete building. The elevator is one of those that you have to jump up and down in, to get it to start. The princess is a tall woman, full of temperament, energy, and good cheer. She has invited three of her friends to join us. They all spent time in prison after the war; she did, too; her husband died there. The Ceausescu years left them with far less sinister a memory than the years 1947-50, after the Communists took power. Expropriations, incarcerations; this was when the great purges took place. However, they have no thought of recrimination; nor of claiming the few acres that have been promised to them in compensation. They judge King Michael severely. Just think! None of his four daughters, whom he raised in Switzerland, speaks Romanian. Curiously, it is rather the young people in this country, the students, who are royalist.

The princess made an exquisite lunch: delicate hors d'oeuvres, and a sweet, cream-colored chicken pilaf. She lays out the plates and the dishes on small tables that she places in front of our armchairs, saying, "Excuse me, but my servants have been on holiday since 1948." A great devourer of books, she complains that it is so hard to get anything new from France except for lousy novels. She pulls two examples from the shelf, books that received the most important literary prizes in Paris last year. "Eight hundred pages, this one. It's about a case of incest, which is never consummated. After all that we have lived through, do you think we are interested in this nonsense? Don't you have anything to say, in France?"

Eugene Ionesco enjoys an international renown, which obscures the accomplishments of his compatriot and predecessor Ion Luca Caragiale. This satirist, descended from a family of actors, wrote plays worthy of Labiche, as early as the second half of the 19th century. Burlesque exploitation of the commonplace and of verbal absurdity did not start in 1950. In 1878, *One Stormy Night* ridiculed the new bourgeoisie of Bucharest. Grotesque characters are caught in the act of committing everyday offences, the comic stupidity of ordinary chattering, revealing the parasitic language in which people talk without saying anything, showcases all the clichés, and underscores the vacuity of daily life. The theater of Caragiale proves that humor and derision are a constant of the Romanian genius, if not a speciality and a vital elixir for this so often martyrized country.

Between Caragiale and Ionesco came another son of Romania, Samuel Rosenstock; under the name of Tristan Tzara, he was the first great Romanian writer in French. In 1916, the capital of international pacifism was Zurich; and there, this twenty-year-old launched the most fantastic literary revolution of modern times (and the most iconoclastic company of all times). At the Voltaire cabaret, in Spielgasse (Games Street!). Dada: a name selected by opening the dictionary at random. Dada: a ridiculous onomatopoeia, and a challenge to the old culture and the society which, while calling itself "humanistic," had just plunged Europe into war.

In 1920, Tzara and his friends launched the *New French Review*, igniting a noisy and gestural reaction in the tidy and refined Paris. During a public event one morning, Tzara read an article from a newspaper, while the sound of an alarm drowned out his voice. "I wanted, quite simply, to show that my appearance on the stage, my figure, my movements should be enough to inspire people's curiosity, and that what I was saying had, fundamentally, no importance."

The historians of literature regard surrealism as the natural continuation of Dada, but they forget that the latter rejoins the conventional world of written literary text. All the Dada events, still astonishing today, were read in public, shouted, and danced. What counted for Tzara was not the work itself, but the physical pleasure of taking part in its creation. The famous sentence: "Thought is formed by the mouth" is not only the poet's assertion of spontaneity and automatism, it also implies a contempt for, and a rejection of, paper. That is a philosophy and an esthetics whose insolence can be well-appreciated in a country where that commodity is so hard to come by. Theater seems to be much more alive than the novel, in Romania these days.

Diametrically opposite of Tzara and Ionesco, free from humor and imbued, on the contrary, with pathos, is another example of this fertile interbreeding of two cultures. His fame as a historian of religions and as a mythologist continues to overshadow Mircea Eliade's romantic writing. However, anyone who has read his two splendid books of memoirs, *Promises of the Equinox* and *Harvests of the Solstice* (Gallimard), knows how much his fiction meant to him. All his life, it pained him not to be recognized as a writer. At the age of 17, while still in school in Bucharest, he began his first narrative, *The Novel of a Myopic Teenager.* It was never published, except for some extracts in magazines, and the manuscript was lost until recently, when it was found in an attic in the Romanian capital.

Seldom has a teenager spoke so clearly about adolescence. He was ambitious to rectify a shortcoming: all the young people described in the novels that he had read seemed false and contrived: described from an adult's perspective. In his work, we have an almost clinical self-portrait of a seventeen year old boy and, at the same time, the portrait of his schoolmates, as well as an overall picture of literary youth in Bucharest in the years 1920-1925 — the era of jazz and *Le Garçonne,* Victor Margueritte's famous and scandalous French novel, whose crude eroticism inspired Eliade's pages about his visits to the brothel. It is a sign of the authenticity of the story, the incredible jumble of intellectual plans and physical pruritus, meditations on existence and pangs over virginity, yearning for God and for sex, all tangled into a passionate time bomb.[†††]

It is more than a novel, it is a journal. We see a high-school student setting out to create a novel but, due to his inability to create believable characters, settling for a day-by-day report of impressions — the notes that Eliade himself had recorded since the age of fourteen, many of which he later admitted were directly transcribed into his first work of fiction. The great drama of Mircea, at that time, was the inadequacy of his will compared to his ambition. A typical adolescent drama, fighting every minute, and related here with passion and precision. The student wished to be strong, independent, pure of spirit in striving toward the most sublime goals. Every morning he would give himself a solemn lecture. And at the end of every day, he had to admit that he had behaved in a lazy and cowardly way, that he had wasted his time, that he was nothing but a dreamer, no better than the other boys in school, and like them blaming the stupidity of the curriculum and the mediocrity of the instructors, whereas he should have blamed his own spinelessness. Sometimes he is tempted to run away, to head out along the Danube and recreate himself through adventure, like Panait Istrati; but he immediately abandons the idea, knowing he hasn't the courage and being unwilling to abandon his book collection. "I am just a teenager like all the others. I will never succeed in life. . . Don't I know better than anybody that I am sentimental, weak, with no will power?"

Floreshti

Radu Ionescu, a famous art critic, had promised us a surprise. He has fine face, well sculpted, and an acute gaze behind metal-rimmed glasses. He is one of the most disillusioned Romanians whom we met; and he never mentions the revolution of 1989 without adding the epithet "so-called." He is sharp and intelligent. Under his somewhat dry

Floreşti: the old Cantacusino palace

exterior, one can sense a person who has been deeply hurt; under this skepticism that does not seem to leave room for any lingering naivety, one senses that the wounds are still open. We learned that he had been imprisoned for over a year, under the old regime, for a crime that would not likely be treated with any more indulgence by the new, to judge from his absolute lack of confidence in the country's modernization. His face only lit up when he was talking to us about this "surprise," a discovery, a secret that he wanted to share with us.

We leave by car, heading north, up the valley of Prahova. After an hour on the main road, we take a country lane and arrive at the village of Floreshti. Radu signals to the driver to stop in front of a house erected at the entry to a park. An immense wall surrounds the park. One day while he was exploring the area, he says, he saw this wall and was intrigued by how long it was. Suspecting that this must be some old seignorial property, he went in.

Beyond the house, we see several modern buildings, cheap and uninteresting, and, sitting on benches here and there, a half-dozen old men in pyjamas. The place has been transformed into an old-age home. However, at the four corners of what's left of the lawn, stand enormous stone vases, carved reliefs of animals and plants, and neo-baroque garlands, items that could not have been commissioned by the Office of Public Assistance. What princely splendors had we stumbled upon? We go around the buildings. In the middle of a meadow that has returned to the wild state, emerging from the sea of grasses (where a cow was taking full pleasure), here was Radu Ionescu's secret: a square edifice, grand and beautiful, and almost intact on the exterior (although it was clear at first glance that this was a ruin). Like a Florentine palace, the building rests on a base of horizontal embossings.

"I discovered it by chance, a year and half ago. No art history book, no guide mentions it. Nobody knows about it. I was able to establish that a prince of the Cantacuzino family had been building it; he was interrupted by the First World War, and during the Second War a bomb damaged the interior."

Never did a ruin more ostentatiously celebrate the alliance of grandeur and abandonment. Six double twin pillars grace the façade that faces what was to be the garden; it is crowned by a richly carved cornice. The roof had been terraced. The geometrical regularity of the horizontal and vertical lines, the severe harmony of the ensemble suggest a taste for antiquity; but the scale of the building, the square form, the long portico pierced by shadow evoke the residences built by the English colonists in the Indies. I saw many of these frozen constructions in Calcutta, which the vicissitudes of history, decrepitude or incompletion imbued with life, with an intense poetry. Add here the pasture and the cattle, the isolation and the rustic surroundings, and you will have an idea of how this monument appears now. Designed as a neo-classical temple, with the glory of symmetry and reason, it has been transformed into sublime absurdity. The meticulously carved bas-reliefs, the luxuriant capitals, the ribbons of stone carved into seashells and foliage, clash with the ruin of the building and contribute to the delirious metamorphosis of the grand original plan.

The sides of the palace feature open arcades. Trees have pushed their branches through the empty windows. Greek majesty and Victorian reserve, thwarted by the expansion of the vegetation. The main façade is splitting, and the two sides pieces lean outward while the midsection tilts back. The monumental gate stands like a triumphal arch. Two grooved columns support a complicated entablature. Between the round vault of the door and the architrave, two angels in bas-relief display the escutcheon and the crown of Cantacuzino.

Above the gate, one sees only the sky, as the designer intended; from the inside, too, one sees the sky, now that the interior has collapsed. The staircase that was to lead to the entrance was never built, or has collapsed. We climb some blocks of stone and cross the threshold. A kind of wild garden of thistles and brambles is growing among the rubble and enormous cracked flagstones in what would have been the gracious apartments of one of Romania's richest and most powerful lords. The construction must have been pretty far advanced; you can see large pipes inside the gaping walls, apparently the heat ducts.

A poignant union of beauty and disaster; a surreal abortion of a rigorous plan; more poetic in its demise than the completed version could ever have been. It's tempting to see the grand Floreshti Palace as an emblem of the national destiny. It is a classical temple recreated by Gaudi as an opera set.

Snagov: the church (next page) (F.F.)

Relaxing in Snagov

Norbert and Svetlana take us along for a weekend in Snagov, to the little lakeside house they are renting. Snagov, some 20 miles from Bucharest, is a village of fishermen where people from the capital go to relax. But to qualify it as a "vacation place" or "resort" would give the Western reader a very misleading impression of this handful of charming, simple bungalos.

The place has hardly changed since the time when Panaït Istrati praised it as the "oasis of love in the vast Wallachian plain that drowns Bucharest like a desert." The same solitary forest, the same scrubby little islands, the same matt of reeds crowns this pond; the same frog choirs, and "here and there, a water lily, king of purity," which "proudly stands watch over the solitude of the lake." Only this plant, with its broad palettes spread flat on the water, has invaded the shoreline, covering several yards of the shallow water with such dense vegetation that it has become almost impossible to go for a swim. In Ceausescu's day, apparently, the lakeside was kept clear; now, nature has taken over. The new power's negligence is even more harmful in the agricultural sector. I heard that insecticides are no longer distributed, as they were under Ceausescu. Colorado beetles destroyed the potato harvest that year, making people fear a famine in the winter.

An asphalt road cuts through the village, which consists of two lines of houses sprinkled among the trees at the edge of the lake. Paths lead from this road down to the water's edge. The little garden that surrounds Norbert and Svetlana's house stops where the wall of reeds starts. Nothing could be more exquisite than this retreat protected by a palisade, whose uprights are far enough apart to allow one to see through (as everywhere in the Romanian countryside, where the desire to fence off one's courtyard does not stifle the interest in being convivial. Here there is only wood, grass, water, peace, happiness. An old boat, grounded among the weeds, is returning to the elements. The remains of a floating dock, similarly overcome by the energetic vegetation, is now used only for sunbathing. The cottage itself is delightful. The three or four rooms have rudimentary furniture that harmonizes with the freshness of the landscape. The bathroom has nothing but a

Bran Castle: XIII century
related to Vlad Ţepeş/The Impaler/Dracul/Dracula

wash basin; there is a tap, connected to an electric pump, but for mysterious reasons, the day we got there, not a drop was forthcoming; so we went to the neighbors', with buckets.

Crossing the sole street of the village takes you a hundred years back. Behind the fences, one sees huts, shanties, houses, and sheds, all decorated with a simple and sure taste that has not deteriorated under the ambitions of industrial civilization. There are still a few authentic thatched cottages, crouching under their thick roofs of straw. The only building for public use is an orthodox church, with white façade, preceded by an alley of trees. There are no stores. On Sunday morning, an open cart loaded with hundreds of gilded round loaves of bread, is parked at the main crossroads. The peasant stands quietly beside his horse; he doesn't seem to be in any hurry to complete his sales. Romanian bread is generally a treat.

It takes a good half hour's walk through a splendid forest to reach the public landing, at another point on this lake with its very sinuous shoreline. Here you can rent a row boat and navigate, between the water lilies, to a small island girded with reeds. This island played a part in the history of Romania. In the 15th century, Vlad Tsepesh (Ţepeş), prince of Wallachia (also known as Vlad the Impaler), beat back the Turks in many heroic battles; he hid his court and his treasure here before waging war on Mahomet II. A monastery, putatively founded by a disciple of Nicodemus, was built on the island in the 14th century. Today, only the church remains; it is traditionally orthodox in style, with its walls of brick and its round bell-towers, and a gigantic priest who emerges from the presbytery to verify that we are not disembarking on his territory clad immodestly in swim suits. The little island seems deserted, except for the priest and the customary cow in the grass. It is this loneliness, this silence, this green and liquid serenity that gives the sanctuary of Snagov its allure, more than the architecture, which has been too often altered since medieval times.

We were exploring this tiny Eden when our attention was drawn by a burst of chattering and cackling of birds: at the edge of the water, behind the trees, a pig sty, a laundry line and a few animals indicated the presence of an informal farmstead. A charming boy appeared in the clearing, tanned and tow-headed, bright as a sunbeam. He came over to meet us, and followed us around for a bit; he seemed to enjoy having his picture taken. He led us toward a thorny bush and picked a few blackberries for us. He said his name was Liviu.

At the center of the island stands a grave; but there is no marker, no inscription, no ornament. "The tomb of Dracula," Liviu declared, giving us a sidewise glance to see whether this comment would have its desired effect. By "Dracula," he meant the 15th century prince, called the Impaler because of his spectacular excesses. He spread so much terror that he came to be called *Dracul*, the Devil. Actually, Vlad III of Wallachia was a valorous warrior, who died in 1478 in the war against the Turks. The humanistic Italian Enea Silvio Piccolomini, who become pope under the name of Pius II, contributed to the creation of the black legends about this prince; in his *Commentarii*, he castigated his cruel excesses as much as he praised his bold and effective military initiatives. As for Dracula, "the Monster of the Carpathians" who sucked his victims' blood, that is a late literary invention, as the English novelist Bram Stoker pointed out (1897). The fictional character eroded the reputation of the historical character and, for a hundred years, popular belief has identified the hero with the monster.

On our way back to our rowboat, we turned to say good-bye to Liviu. But he had disappeared, as inexplicably as he had first appeared — leaving us to wonder whether we had imagined him, whether he was some folkloric incarnation, the island's first resident, an elf who was here before Vlad and Dracula?

We returned the following day. No sign of Liviu. No sign of anybody. We rowed around the island, half thinking we might surprise him sitting on a lily pad among the nymphs. If he was there, we did not see him. . .

* Mircea Cartarescu, *The Dream*, Paris: Editions Climats. Translated by Helene Lenz.

** Apollinaire already noted (*The Eleven Thousand Rods* chapter 1): "Bucharest is a beautiful city where the East seems to blend with the West."

† At the end of 1995, the restoration of the royal palace as well as of the library seemed to be making great progress.

†† Avenue of the Victory of Socialism, under Ceausescu, was renamed to Freedom Boulevard.

††† Full of an enthusiasm that, according to his friend Mihaï Sebastian's *Journal: 1935-1944* (published in 1996), led him to take up with the Iron Guard, a fascistic and anti-Semitic movement of the 1930's-1940's.

From the capital city we headed for the mountains, the steep, austere peaks of Transylvania. The first stop along the way, heading north
out of Bucharest, is the château of Mogoshoaia. Built in 1702 by prince
Constantin Brancoveanu, it offers a good example of the composite
style (called "Brancovan") that was born at the end of the 17th century
as a fusion of the Eastern Byzantine and Italian Renaissance. Openwork balustrades, Venetian loggias, trefoil arcades enliven with their
gracious motifs the massive deep red construction. The most beautiful
façade faces out over the lake: an open gallery with twisted columns,
richly decorated on their capitals. The château seems abandoned; spi-
ders weave their wonders across the parquet floors.

Prince George Bibescu, a cousin of the two Bibescus who were
friends of Proust (Emmanuel and Antoine), bought it in 1911 as a gift for
his wife, Martha Lahovary. George, unlike his cousins, was coarse and
brutish, a true lout. Martha said of their marriage that it was like giving a Stradivarius to a monkey. The gift of Mogoshoaia was meant as a
reparation granted to the one who was said to be the most beautiful
and the most refined woman in Romania. After the Great War, she
wrote novels and volumes of memoirs (in French), including *Au Bal avec
Marcel Proust*; she rivaled her cousin the countess Anna de Noailles

The Brâncoveanu House of Mogoşoaia (1688-1714)

(born Brancoveanu, and the stunningly beautiful daughter of a Romanian father and a Turkish mother), for literary and fashionable primacy in Paris. In the very same years, the 1920's, Panaït Istrati started to publish his books. Thus, two aristocrats of high birth and one plebeian and impecunious Bohemian inaugurated the era of Romanian francophony.

In the long run, it's talent that won out over the privileges of birth; the most interesting achievement of the princess Bibescu was undoubtedly the restoration of Mogoshoaia*, which took seventeen years. The building was in disrepair when she took it over; she hired Italian masons under the direction of the architect Domenico Rupolo and she traveled to Venice, to Fortuny, to buy the fabrics to decorate the salons. Then, although she often traveled and had a beautiful apartment on the Île de Saint-Louis in Paris, she continued to make long stays at her Romanian residence and gave receptions there, even during the war, when Mogoshoaia became a refuge for the intellectuals of Bucharest.[1]

Martha Bibescu did not leave Romania permanently until 1945, after the Russian occupation. The deserted building now preserves no trace of her passage, and it seems likely that it will fall into the same ruin from which she had extracted it. The motionless lake, the garden swathed in silver threads, and the silence of the forgotten countryside symbolize the fiasco of a dream of elegance and beauty incompatible with the harsh reality of today. It was already purely a dream, on behalf of Constantin Brancoveanu, to try to adapt the style and the tone of Venice to the environment of Wallachia. And now, nothing remains of this Utopia but the anachronistic and doomed decor of a Romanized palace from Istanbul.

Between Bucharest and Brashov lies the mountain resort of Sinaia, where Carol I built Pelesh Castle in the 1880's, an amusing example of the pseudo-historical and frankly kitsch style that was so much in vogue, at the end of the 19th century, all over Central Europe and especially in Hungary. A heterogeneous assemblage of stone and wood, it is an absurd amalgam of Byzantine and Gothic elements, a combination of pointed roofs, crenellated turrets and ogival stained glass windows, the building is as ornate on the interior as it is on the exterior.

The town of Brashov, nestled in its circle of mountains, introduces us to Transylvania, ground of passage and mixing where Romanian,

Magyars, Germans, Gypsies met and continue to mix. The Germans arrived in the 13th century, invited by King Geza II of Hungary to assist in his resistance to the Turks and the Mongols. They were accorded various freedoms and privileges, and settled in for the long term. Brashov, which was called formerly Kronstadt ("city of the crown"), was one of their strongholds. It still preserves a certain Germanic character, Saxon rigor and bourgeois severity that even contact with the East has hardly succeeded to soften. The evangelical church (known as the Black Church because of smoke damage from a fire in 1689 that singed its powerful buttresses and massive tower), resembles a fortress. Under the high Gothic vaults, the inscription "I know and I believe" underscores the virtues of a recumbent figure lying in his armor and his helm. This is a solid citadel, the double bastion of the Lutheran faith and Western reason: so much so that the splendid Turkish carpets hanging on the walls look like trophies; far from hinting at the ambiguous delights of Asia, they proclaim victory over the Infidels, and the glory of the God of Rome.

Germany left an even deeper mark in the chain of fortified churches erected between Brashov, Sighishoara and Sibiu. These extraordinary constructions all display pretty much the same design. A kremlin of high ramparts surrounds the sanctuary. Inside the enclosure thus defined and barricaded against invaders from the East were residential buildings and food storage sheds. In the event of danger, theentire village would take refuge behind the walls, ready to withstand a siege.

We come across the first of these fortified churches, with its austere and inexpugnable aspect, in Harman, shortly after leaving Brashov. The guard greets us with "Grüss Gott!" (as un-Romanian as can be.) He tells us, in German, the history of this Saxon village. Founded in the 13th century, it remains Germanic today, at least in terms of language. The church, protected by its surrounding walls, was besieged 47 times but was never taken. Balconies with wooden balustrades, staircases, and footbridges connect the rooms inside the walls. Of the 1200 Germans who lived in the village until Ceausescu's downfall, only 250 remain today.

Clear, simple, stark, the image of rectitude and of the mental ro-
bustness that inspired the Reformation, the church is preceded by a
carillon. The only ornamentation at the entrance is provided by the
ogival beams of the doorframe itself. A rough wooden floor, strewn
with rough carpets. The German taste for discipline is shown in the
positioning of the seats. The stalls of the transepts, perpendicular to
the altar, have backrests; they are reserved for the men. The women
don't get any backrest; they sit together on plain benches, opposite the
altar, the older women in the first rows. Does this discrimination mean
that the men should be rewarded as hard workers, while the women,
daughters of Eve, will never finish expiating the sins of their gender?

Prejmer, another Saxon village, is just a few miles away. It has a
double circular enclosure, and long access passage defended by a series
of portcullises. Of all the fortified churches in Transylvania, this one is
the best-preserved. Three stories of cells line the interior walls. There
are 272 rooms, each one numbered. The villagers kept their provisions
there, and were ready to take refuge there at the first alarm. These
rooms open onto a wooden gallery. The covered walkway is still us-
able: you can walk all the way around the enclosing wall and admire
the astonishing system of beams and frames. Trap doors in the floor
overhanging the exterior allowed the besieged to pour boiling pitch on
their enemies. A long tunnel, it seems, led to an exit far outside the enclosure, making it possible to organize an occasional supply run. The
guard showed us the entrance to the tunnel.

As in Harman, the church is Gothic, bare, austere. The hierarchy
of the seating even stricter, and goes by age as well as gender. Men and
women occupy of separate benches. The left transept is reserved for
young men and young ladies (in two distinct groups), the right transept is for the elderly. The middle-aged kept to the nave. The organ is
above the altar and, on the pillars, there are panels giving the numbers
of the psalms of the day. Order, rigor, and subordination of the individual to the law, a meticulous announcement of the program of the day's
service: the Protestant ideal has managed to stay intact in the land of
compromise that is multinational Romania, multi-ethnic and multi-
religious.

It was in Homorod, halfway between Brashov and Sighishoara,
that we heard the most complete history of these church-fortresses and

Harman: fortified church (F.F.)

the Saxon communities whose permanence is so surprising. Here, the church is built almost in the middle of the village, in the center of a vast esplanade surrounded by the peasants' farms, their rustic houses painted yellow or green, connected by a fence, with a gate which opens on the court. The enclosing wall is shut. Children of the nearby orphanage go to look for the guard at one end of the village. He arrives on an old black bicycle. Big, powerful, wearing a straw hat, very dignified, he bears with good nature the seventy years of an existence that we suppose cannot have been too rich with experience and emotion. After greeting us in German, he first lets us into the enclosure, flanked by four bastions in the corners, then into the church, through a raised door that leads us directly to the balcony of the second story. The church dates from 1270. The baroque altar and the organ go back to 1784, like the paintings at the front of the balcony (curiously floral), they are Mozart's contemporaries. In this pastel décor, on the gray-painted bench, the guard talks to us at length about his life and the life of his village, while we gaze into the empty nave, clear and cold, such a different atmosphere from the warm half-light of an orthodox church.

Few meetings moved us more than this one. Johann Thomé is a German, and he spoke to us in German. His ancestors arrived in the 13th century. They were not Saxons (as the Hungarians indifferently call all Germans). They came from the area between the Rhine and the Moselle. They cleared the forests, established agricultural fields and lived here for seven centuries, with their particular liberties and freedoms, as peaceful colonists. In 1943, all the male subjects aged seventeen to forty were called up by the Wehrmacht. The majority — twenty-eight exactly (we later read their names on commemorative plaque outside the church — were killed in France, in Cherbourg. Those who returned were arrested by the Romanians, and deported to Siberia. According to Johann Thomé, they didn't even know who was Hitler and what was Nazism.

"Before the war, the Germans worked as if they had eternity before them, and prayed as if they were going to die the next day." He said this with tears in his eyes, and we find it easy to believe him. Without realizing it, he gave us the perfect summary of Lutheran morals, which merges with the rule by which he had governed his own life.

He was seventeen in 1945. He fled the village to escape military

Prejmer: fortified enclosure (F.F.)

draft. For five months, he lived in the forest, returning at night to the family home for supplies. He would set out again at dawn, after hugging his mother, his father and his eight year old brother. When the war was over, their land was confiscated by the Romanians. Homorod then had 800 Germans, 200 Romanians, and 200 Gypsies. In 1989, only 300 Germans remained. Ceausescu had not allowed them to emigrate; and as soon as they were given passports, they left for Germany, Austria, France, or Canada. Now the village has only fifteen Germans, the oldest, distributed among five families; and they live among 400 Hungarians, 300 Romanians and a good thousand Gypsies.

In 1989, the State co-operative lost its monopoly, and the land was redistributed: 25 acres per Romanian, 12 acres per German. This was a double injustice, since the Germans were the better farmers. Between 1980 and 1990, they lived on 200 grams of bread per day, with a half-liter of cooking oil and a half-kilo of sugar per month. "No one who didn't live through it can understand the hard times we had under communism." But there is no bitterness in his voice, no grudge against the Communists nor against the Romanians, only the deep melancholy of a man who is one of the last fifteen survivors of a community that will soon disappear, after having enjoyed seven centuries of honest, robust and glorious existence. He tells us all this calmly, at the height of his natural majesty. From his great, round face with its broad forehead and double chin emanate benevolence and forgiveness. He is like the local chief, and does not wish to waste his time in complaints or recriminations, at the hour when his tribe is dying out, when their language will soon be a dead language.

There is another church in the village, originally built for the orthodox Romanians. This one is used in turn by the Germans of the reformed church and by Hungarian catholics. The Lutheran pastor comes every three months from Sighishoara, the catholic priest comes every three or four weeks from Hungary. We go down into the nave. Three painted panels decorate the pulpit: a sower, a cherub holding up the Bible in a ray of light spouting out of its heart, and a Bible posed on a rock. The organ, prettily made, is fed by foot-pedal bellows. You have to hold onto a bar placed horizontally on two posts, and press each pedal alternately. Johann Thomé enjoys showing us how the bellows function. The organ is in working condition, and the interior of the church, in spite of the infrequent services, is impeccably clean. Be-

hind a door, a ruined apse remains of the first sanctuary. In the half-
light we can make out very faded frescos; they must have been very
beautiful. A crucifixion, and a pietà.

To finish, Johann invites us to go to the top of the tower, from
which we can appreciate the star-shaped layout of the village, German
order, German efficiency, the rational organization of the cultivated
land, and the stone and tile of the houses (instead of the cob and thatch
of the Moldovan regions). More solidity, less charm, as in Catsa,
Drausheni (north of Homorod), or in Biertan, beyond Sighishoara.

The fortified church of Biertan, one of most beautiful, stands inside a triple enclosure of towers and bastions. It is reached via a covered external staircase. Here, too, we were greeted in German, here too
the Gothic nave strikes us with its clarity and starkness, here too the
program of worship is in German, here too is a monument listing the
names of the German soldiers killed during the two world wars, and
here too, no doubt, the few rare descendants of the great Germanic adventure in Transylvania feel themselves being drowned by the Gypsies
who come from the East.

Their ancestors repulsed the Tatars and the Turks; now, they have
to give in to the Gypsy invasion. The Dacic wars, by which Emperor
Trajan secured the possession of what is now Romania, ended in the
year 107 AD. Dacia was Roman until 275: less than two centuries,
which is not long, compared to the seven centuries of German colonization. But the Romans and the Germans had the same civilizing virtues,
the same aptitude for work and organization; and perhaps, still today,
the various people that make up Romania are held together only thanks
to the cohesion and the unity imprinted by these messengers of the
Western *logos* over the confused, the profuse, the centrifugal and de-
lightfully ambiguous *Mitteleuropa*.

Before we arrive at Sighishoara, we make a detour to Odor-
heiul, an entirely Hungarian town. I check the bookshop: not a single Romanian book, everything is in Magyar.

As for Sighishoara, its name has alternated between the German Schässburg and Hungarian Segesvár. The lanes of this small
city climb a steep hill, and unusually for Romania, it looks like one
of those medieval villages full of mysterious turns and recesses. The
lower city is dreadful, parceled out in lugubrious low-income housing

developments; but if you go up to the higher part of the city you can sit in the shade of a chestnut tree, on the other side of the back entry to what was the citadel. Everything is uneven, sinuous, asymmetrical, unimaginably picturesque and a respite from socialist claims to rationality. If this were a lime tree rather than a chestnut, you could easily imagine you were under Schubert's *Lindenbaum*, although here is no inviting inn to visit.

A high and massive tower with four pinnacles dominates the plaza. A monumental clock, four stories high. It is worth the trouble to climb up, to examine the wheels and the ornaments of this extremely refined mechanism. Seven figurines, three feet tall, appear in turn each day under the dial. The change takes place at midnight. From the top of the tower, you have a beautiful view out over the brown tiled roofs, pointed pinions, iron arrows and standards planted along the ridge tops of the campaniles. One would expect the medieval explosion of a brass band of horns, bells and saqueboutes, but the tower remains mute in this quiet city.

A covered staircase, built entirely of wood and some 1000 feet long, a wonder of 17th century carpentry, leads us to the top of the hill. The Gothic church is not particularly interesting, but, behind the church, a very pleasant cemetery stretches along the spur that extends above the plain, with a labyrinth of alleys leading in every direction. Half-hidden under a tumble of greenery, nearly all the tombs bear German names, even the most recent. I also see, here and there, the Masonic triangle, compass and eye.

Close to the Clock Tower, there is a restaurant in a beautiful yellow house, where the prince Vlad Dracul, Vlad the Impaler is supposed to have been born here in 1431. If Dracula turns up here, what part of Romania might have remained untouched by his sanguinary appetites and crimes? This would seem to have been a natural den for him. A touch of Satanism completes the romantic allure of the escarpment, the dark and twisting streets of Sighishoara, and it isn't hard to imagine owls roosting (or bats, or vampires) under the eaves, in the dark recesses.

The only hotel in town was full, so we were directed to a motel that had been opened recently, five miles away, very new, a modern establishment, in a building that was really "frumoasa." "Frumos" means

Biertan: fortified enclosure (F.F.)

"beautiful," and in Romanian, the adjective takes a diphthong in its feminine form, a delicate dilation that expresses the superiority of the gender of Venus. We should diverge for a moment to ponder this way of distinguishing beauty by form, the plenitude of the form. *Frumos* comes from the Latin *formosus* (which also gave us the Italian *formoso*). Romania, by giving the name of "beautiful" to that which has a well-defined "form," shows its Latin roots, preferring robust contours. Theophilus Gautier would have liked this country, he who has the narrator of *Mademoiselle de Maupin* say that he like three things: "éclat, solidity, and color," and "Never fog nor vapor, never anything dubious and floating. My sky has no clouds, or, if it has any, they are solid and cut with a chisel, made from the marble blocks fallen from the statue of Jupiter." All vagueness is excluded from such an ideal of plastic vigor, all the fuzziness of prayer, of religious meditation. "There is no place there for the weakness and dreams of Christian art." Later on, we will see how Brancusi, the sculptor with a mystical bent, remained true to the Romanian worship of the *frumos*, in spite of his attraction to the supernatural and his curiosity for the beyond, to the understanding of beauty as finite volumes, clear, polished: objects of metal or marble, whose silhouette describes a simple contour, without fussiness or distraction.

The modern "beauty," alas! seems to have taken on a different meaning, for the motel in question, isolated in the midst of the countryside, was unfinished and rather "unformed;" it looked less like an honest lodging for travelers than an assassins' lair. We seemed to be the only customers; and, in front of the door, to greet us, was a group of individuals with dark and sinister looks. Pure imagination? Too much thinking about the legends of Dracula? But why were windowpanes missing from our rooms, if not to allow, in the dark of night, the flight of ghouls and merry renegades escaped from the dark procession of the Impaler? Even without allowing ourselves to get carried away by these absurd terrors, we had trouble getting to sleep, due to a more commonplace reality, the poor condition of the plumbing. The toilet dripped with an exasperating insistence; and heaven forbid you try to flush it; it ran for a quarter of an hour, without stopping, like Niagara Falls.

I regret that we only once passed through Cluj, and too quickly at that. The former Klausenburg preserves the grid-like layout of the streets and a great square piazza, toward which all the avenues converge, from the years of Saxon colonization; it was later Magyarized. This is the second most important town of Transylvania, after Brashov. The sizeable Hungarian minority is very active, and has its own schools, newspapers, and posters on the kiosks; but the era of protests and disorder that shook this area after Transylvania was joined to Romania in 1920, seems to be finished. Hungary has recognized the intangibility of the borders that were established by the Treaty of the Trianon; in exchange, Romania accords the Magyar community considerable privileges. We were warmly received in Cluj by Liliana and a small group of teachers, who made us all the more sorry to have so little time to spare.

Some 50 miles to the east, we were able to stop a little longer at Tirgu Muresh, the principal town of the Hungarian autonomous area of Muresh. This town of 230,000 inhabitants preserves beautiful evidence of the Magyar culture. The Hungarians are still majority there but, in the bookshops, Romanian books and Hungarian books share the display space.

At the Continental Hotel, ugly but comfortable, a friend of Norbert's joins us. Young Ildico is neither as fair-haired nor as Venus-like as the *frumoasa* Svetlana, but she has plenty of character, and she represents a no less attractive sample of the Romanian woman. Actually, she is Hungarian. She wears a short skirt, with her hair cut short, pink shoes with high heels, and a smart, decided air. She teaches English at Ocna Muresh, not far from the farm where her parents still grow corn and raise hens and pigs.

She promises to take us to lunch the next day at the farm, impromptu, since they do not have a telephone. For now, we eat at an Italian restaurant close to the hotel. This is an innovation, for Romania. The standard modern decor, and good food — which could be excellent if Italian chefs were in charge of the kitchen. Tempted by the *bistecca fiorentina*, we ordered it rare. It was no use; they delivered it cooked to death like a roast of veal, massacring a naturally tender and tasty meat. There were quite a few foreign customers, as in Sighishoara. One might predict that, when Romania recovers a little credit, the tourists will start to flood in via Transylvania and Bukovina. Bukovina, for the monasteries and the duty to absorb some "culture," Transylvania,

Sighişoara: The Bell Towers and the Old City (F.F.)

Tîrgu Mureş: Stained Glass Panels at the Culture Palace (F.F.)

for its orderliness, cleanliness and other advantages inherited from the Austrian empire. I would bet that Moldova and Dobrogiea, whose indolence are so much more poetic, will attract fewer visitors. The eastern parts of Romania are like the south of Italy: people either fall in love with the region, or they don't trust it. In fact they are strange places, marvelous perhaps, but they don't play by the rules.

In the evening we take a walk along the central square, which is almost a mile long — more like a very broad avenue divided into two traffic corridors separated by a strip of woods. This place bears the beautiful name of Trandafirilor, "Roses." The name is composed of *trandafir*, "rose" (and this is a rose with an indisputably Turkish aroma), and the suffix *ilor*, which marks the genitive plural and is derived from Latin. Actually, the square is suffused with Hungarian elements. Discreetly baroque houses, similar to those one might see in Buda, alternate with Jugendstil façades reminiscent of Pest. The most astonishing

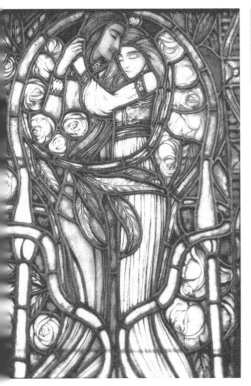

monument is the Palace of Culture, erected early in the 20th century by the architects Komor Marcell and Jakob Deszö. The projecting windows, the corbels, the canopies, the combination of rustic elements and precubist geometry make it a stunning specimen the Secession style. The variety of materials is also typical of this fashion: bronze, marble, glass, wood, brick, glazed ceramic, wrought iron. We propose to visit it the following day.

The interior does not disappoint us, in spite of the reservations expressed by the author of the brochure, a certain Traian Dusha, who may (considering his imperial name) have felt called upon to defend the honor of Dacia against Magyar taste.

The hall is presented in the form of a long passageway, prolonged at each end by a mirror that reflects *ad infinitum* the line of chandeliers and arcades. Six domes, alternatively hemispherical and ellipsoidal, painted in green, brown and patinated gold, punctuate the ceiling.

Black marble pillars from Sweden, sinuous frescos featuring angels in long flowing robes, garlands of flowers, and diffuse light that veils as much as it reveals of this luxury of curves and colors, contribute to the creation of an intimate, ambiguous, voluptuous atmosphere. The staircase, of white marble, is decorated with inserts of stained glass. A portrait of Liszt is featured on the main floor; then comes Erkel, the other Hungarian national composer.

The concert hall, three stories tall, holds close to 800 seats: an enormous figure for the town of Tirgu Muresh that must have been, in 1911, a village of a few tens of thousands of inhabitants. The organ has some 5,000 pipes, making it one of largest in Europe in its day; it fills the space above a futuristic mural. The seats, the fabrics, the lamps, the balustrades, all are in harmony. This is the most complete, the most harmonious, and the best-preserved Art Nouveau ensemble I've seen since the Municipal House of Prague. Tirgu Muresh also has a fine symphony orchestra, which played Bach and Vivaldi in Paris; we heard them rehearsing a contemporary work by Hans Peter Turk, a Romanian of German origin who resides in Cluj.

The Salon of Mirrors should be called Stained Glass, because it has twelve large stained glass panels that throw brilliant colors onto the furniture and carpets. These are works of an exceptional force and beauty. If I said that they made me think of de Mucha, it would detract from the originality of the artist (or artists — no one could tell me who designed them). The Devil Abducting Sarah, the Cradle of Csaba (who would become emperor of Hungary), a naïad swimming; Ildico recounts to us all these old legends from Hungarian folklore. We also see more modest subjects, drafted with the same curvilinear dynamism and same nationalist exaltation — thatched cottages, oxen drawing a cart, flocks of geese — an illustration of the ethnological patrimony of the Szekelys.

Speaking of geese, I finally learned, from Ildico, why they are never available in the restaurants or markets. They are raised privately, not in the State farms, and thus escape the commercial circuits. Moreover, their flesh is considered to be common, coarse. Therefore they wind up in the peasants' plates, never to compete on the public tables with the sorry monopoly of the pork chop.

Noshlac is a village of 400 inhabitants, with dirt roads, fences, and simple houses, like most of Transylvania. The houses stand in a row, bordering the road and backing against their fields. Ildico's parents have six acres, extending from their farm buildings down to a river, the Mureshul.

We open the gate and walk into the courtyard. Ildico's mother doesn't seem too surprised to see us, and she immediately sets to work preparing a monumental dish of *mamaliga*, while we explore the surroundings. There are two houses on the farm, the kitchen and pantry having their own building, as used to be common in many places. The main house has two rooms for sleeping, furnished in the Romanian way with settees that double as beds; there is no sink in the kitchen and no bath in the main house. They draw water from the well, and bathe outside. The space between the two buildings is used to store firewood. Around the sides, there is a lean-to for the four pigs, a sheepfold with six sheep, a hen house and a bin for storing corn, along with various workshops. And lots of geese and hens.

In the fields, they grow corn, wheat and sunflowers, and in the vegetable garden they have tomatoes, cabbage, potatoes, peppers, and squash. The family is quite self-sufficient; they only buy their bread and sugar, and they eat meat only on occasion. They make their soap with caustic soda and lard, and cheese from the milk of their ewes. They have their sunflower seeds pressed in the village to make oil. The father was out the day we visited. He built these houses himself; they are brick on the outside, and concrete on the inside. He's planning to build a baker's oven out of brick so they can use their own flour. In the pantry, I see a pile of potatoes, jars of tomato sauce, sacks full of wool, and bottles of a very light wine, which they make themselves. Behind the main house is a corn shed, with an electric mill. They make jam and preserves for the winter using their own fruits and vegetables.

Ildico gets more wood for the fire, still dressed in her pink spike heels and miniskirt. Then, while the *mamaliga* gently simmers on the stove, she gathers in her arms a heavy pile of blankets and sheepskins. Asking us to follow her, she leads us out the back door and down a little path, beyond the fields, to a small clearing looking out over the river.

"Why don't you relax here in the sun, until the food is ready," she says to Norbert, in Romanian. First, she lays out the blankets on the grass and then, to make it more comfortable for us, she adds the thick sheepskins. This rustic nest being suitably feathered, she then goes

back to her domestic tasks. A "modern," independent woman, bearing no resemblance to a Turkish odalisque, Ildico still preserves nevertheless a particular regard for the male sex, a reverence full of special attentions. She was married, no longer is, and has a young daughter who is now bouncing up and down in her cradle, next to the grandmother who watches her while stirring the pot and performing other rites essential for the success of the *mamaliga*.

We eat in the young woman's room, between the dresser, the TV and the settees, which forces her continually to go back and forth to the kitchen. Her mother does not eat with us; as in Sicily, she remains in the kitchen while receiving foreigners. Ildico speads a tablecloth and brings out of the cupboard dishes which must not be used every day. We are served an exquisite cabbage soup to start; then the *mamaliga*, accompanied by mushrooms that we had bought on a sidewalk in Tirgu Muresh and cleaned with water from the well; and for dessert, grapes and strawberries gathered from the arbor. All of this was accompanied by the light domestic red wine. Ildico made a point of observing the old-fashioned ceremonial code for us; when we asked her for salt, she went to the kitchen for the salt carton and then filled a china salt shaker that had been in the cupboard, and apparently had not been filled since her marriage.

No contrast could be more startling, as we left this village with its patriarchal morals and traditional hospitality, than to pass by the factory at Copsha Mica, on the road for Sibiu. They make lampblack there, in buildings the color of coal, enormous and hideous constructions dumped right in the middle of a green valley, like a Marxist allegory on the victory of industry over nature, of human creativity over the gifts of God.

Cioran and His Hometown

Finally, we come to a large Romanian city that has not been made ugly, disfigured, massacred! One enters Sibiu with inexpressible relief: the narrow streets, the arched passages, the old houses, the town square bordered by a palace with peaked roofs, the entire ensemble that is so reminiscent of old Nuremberg has made it intact across the

Transylvanian village

tumult of the centuries. No added constructions, no hideous industrialization. It could be said that the ramparts, the bastions, the watch towers that protected the city against the Turks for so long, and of which important vestiges remain, have also saved Sibiu from the devastation of modernization. This miracle is all the more astonishing since here we seem to be in a corner of Germany; no other Romanian city has retained such a clear Germanic imprint.

Baron Harmann, suffering an unrequited love for the beautiful Gisele, who became the wife of the Hungarian King Stefan I, decided to go into exile. According to legend, he and his people founded a stronghold in 1284, and for centuries it was known as Harmannstadt. In the 18th century, when Transylvania was ceded to Austria, Baron Samuel de Bruckenthal became governor of the city. He was a big (although perhaps not expert) collector of artwork, books, and coins, and he built the beautiful Viennese Baroque palace that frames one end of the town square; this is now the oldest museum in Romania and is still named for the noble Austrian. The canvases are not necessarily the best, and some of the attributions appear doubtful, but one can get an idea of the Masters whom an enlightened amateur, the contemporary of Mozart, might find interesting: the Italians Titian, Andrea del Sarto, and Guido Reni, the French Bourdon and Oudry, and landscape and animal paintings from Flanders and Holland.

Sibiu is beautiful and mysterious, with its twisting streets, secret staircases, invisible galleries dating from the time when the Turkish threat oppressed the German colony. The city still presents a severe, sad aspect. The people are reserved. Prudence and circumspection! If the city is so well preserved, if order and cleanliness reign in this labyrinth (which, further east, would have turned into a souk), it must be because the population is more inclined toward conservative practices rather than wasteful? No irony intended; but the comparison between the Saxon mindset and that of the Hungarians and the Romanians, two of the most spontaneous and hospital people in the world, invites one to reflect on the price that one has to pay for a more decent habitat and indisputably better conditions of life.

The Irishman Walter Starkie, who visited these areas toward the end of 1920 and left an amusing account of his voyage[2], met a servant girl named Elsa, stout and solidly built, with fair hair and periwinkle eyes, a true Teuton, and very much convinced of the inferiority of the

Romanians. She explained to the traveler that, in her village, in remembrance of the times when one lived in constant fear of a Turkish or Tatar (the future Hungarians) invasion, the peasants continued to store their provisions in the church. Niches had been made in the wall of the sanctuary and were used to store bacon, sausage and maize. "It would seem," comments Starkie, "that after centuries of hard struggle in a distant land, the sparing and careful Saxon nature degenerated into a mania for hoarding." The food shortage may have put an end to such habits long since, but Sibiu retains a sense of organization, a rejection of carelessness that distinguishes Transylvania from other parts of Romania.

The hotel Imparatul Romanilor [Roman Emperor], close to the town square, is the best we found in Romania: in terms of comfort, the quality of the construction, the solidity of the furniture, and the decorative woodwork in the rooms. A little bit of Germany quality has held on until today. With the dramatic name of the establishment, one could even imagine oneself to be visiting an outpost of the Holy Roman Empire.

The lower city, accessed by covered passages and concealed staircases, is where you'll find the manual trades. We walked into a tannery, smoky and smelly, with an atmosphere that probably has not changed much over the centuries. According to Claudio Magris, who wrote a book on Central Europe and the Balkans,[3] dedicated the most significant chapter to Romania, to the poetry of these Germanic cities (Brashov, Sighishoara, Sibiu). It is a poetry, he says, "of the bourgeois and the artisan," solid and melancholic, obstinate and proud. The competitions between trades, "tanners versus saddlers," are part of this awareness of belonging to an elite. And the uninterrupted influence of the Reformation can be seen in this ideology of work and merit.

A rejection of the haphazard can be seen in the comparison between the well-maintained and severe streets of Sibiu and the poetic dilapidation of Braïla. In literature, I could similarly contrast the styles of the two great French-speaking writers of Romania. As Panaït Istrati reflects the open temperament of the bohemian and the nomad in his easy, fluid, temperamental prose, so Emil Cioran is characterized by his concise, dry, spare style, hoarding and parceling out expressions that are gleaned, contained, corseted. In the time of the Turks, the one would have locked up his provisions in a niche in the church, the other would have pulled a hunk of bread from his accordion and shared it

with his companions met along the road. If we wanted to come to Sibiu, it was less to enjoy its beautiful but morose style than to try to understand the places where Cioran spent his youth and girded his spirit.

Born in a village five miles from Sibiu, he was eleven years old in 1921 when he arrived in the capital of Transylvania, where his father, Emilian, had just been named protopope. From 1924 to 1928, the family lived at 24 *via Tribunei*, a street that is easy to find, perpendicular to the *strada Balcescu* (which starts at the town square and is used as a *corso*). It's a pretty, private house, vaguely baroque, in the same style as many of the old houses in Harmannstadt: four windows in the front, with carvings of winged putti and horse heads, a gate on the right-hand side (the gate is never in the middle of the façade, but on the side; it leads to a side courtyard, from which one enters the house). Yellow walls, a tiled roof, quaint charm: nothing, apparently, to inculcate in the child the black thoughts that would be the undercurrent of his work.

When he was fifteen, he started reading the philosophers — German, mostly, in accordance with the tradition of Harmannstadt (from which he might easily have gone to Berlin rather than Paris). He would carry their treatises out to what remains of the town's bastions, an extremely pleasant place, to tell the truth, a long stretch of grass spreading out in the shade of the rampart, and from there, behind a curtain of trees, you can see a row of little houses, brightly painted. He came here, to such a lovely setting, to imbue himself with Schopenhauer and Nietzsche! He was already proud of his insomnia, which enabled him to feel superior to the sleeping populace, the inert bourgeoisie.

He described his native village, Rashinari, as a pastoral paradise, the loss of which caused his first heartache. Cioran spent his early years under the most favorable circumstances; nobody in Romania grew up with so much in his favor. What a paradox: from a painful, miserable childhood, without a father, without a fixed home, Panaït Istrati derived a boundless confidence in human nature, while Cioran, who was raised in a well-to-do family, surrounded by beauty and having access to the best books, derived from these privileges only a vicious fury of negation. How could such a gloomily destructive thought be born and flourish in such strikingly positive surroundings? Cioran did everything to make us believe that his pessimism spouted out fully armed from his brain, as a quiver full of absolute truths, independent of

Sibiu: the Old City

the experiences and emotions of his youth.

However, *The Book of Lures*, the second of his works (written in Romanian, published in Bucharest in 1936 and translated into French only in 1992), modifies the image of this intractable denigrator that is given by his books written directly in French (starting with the *Precis of Decomposition*). Before the war — he was twenty-five years old in 1936 — he had not yet petrified in nihilism, in the woody rigidity that so thrills some of his readers and aggravates others.

"Strike yourself, slap yourself, whip yourself until you feel the most terrible pains. . . Let everything burn in you, so that pain will never make you soft and slack." Yes, Cioran was young, he was not always mired in pessimism. This short text palpitating with a fresh candor fanned by a youthful taste for excess, is suffused with an exaggerated desire to dissociate himself from the herd and to live in the trance and the dance of a lyric metaphor of the absolute. "Ah, brothers, how much we have to suffer in order to enjoy only one moment of delight!" He's not quoting Nietzsche, but in his exclamatory tone, in the impassioned invocations to his "brothers" and the way he orders them to launch out headlong in "risk," one senses the influence of the great prophet studied, at one time, on the green lawns of Sibiu.

He may have been influenced by some of Nietzsche's epigones, as well. Did Cioran read them? He always tried to give the impression that his thoughts were entirely original, he never revealed his sources; but reading his work, one recognizes a hint of Barrès, of Gide, even of Kipling in those pages where he enumerates the means of achieving an invincible moral fiber? Passion, ecstasy, intoxication, religious epiphany, the will to burn one's life in order to become a god weave through this book in red and flaming threads, and with the ardor of the neophyte, hatred explodes of everything that is measured, mediocre, ordinary, temporal, base.

"Regret for not dying at the zenith of the musical and erotic state teaches us how much we have to lose, by living." The most beautiful pages are devoted to music. Not to the music of musicians, for, when Cioran mentions a composer by name, he falls into banality. Cioran is right never to quote nor to analyze books, and we understand why he usually abstains from commenting on others. Cioran is a poor critic, he lacks this power of empathy that makes it possible to enter into communication and communion with the creative flair of others. He is a

Braşov: The Black Church

thinker, locked up in his own system. When he integrates music into his system, when he resounds with his own internal music instead of resorting to Bach or Mozart, when he exalts music as the abolition of the external world and the disintegration of individual limits into a sonorous and uplifting universality, he is writing not only the best of Cioran, powerful, moving, vital, almost baroque in its flexuous élan, but he is giving us one of the best pages that the universe of sounds has ever inspired in a writer. "What is the art of music, if not a soft chaos where the vertigo is a bliss and the undulations of rapture? . . . I am delighted and weak with joy before the musical mystery that resides in me, that projects its reflections in melodious waves, that takes me apart and

reduces my substance to pure intervals."

Reverberating with these burning phrases, we went to Rashinari, his native village. We made the trip by tram, then an invigorating and delightful 5-mile walk, along the edge of a forest. And we discovered, at the end of the winding road, the most beautiful, the purest village in all Romania, which is saying a lot. And the best-preserved, without nothing to mar the calm slopes of the old steep-slanted roofs, the harmony of the green and pink houses going down the sides of two hills to meet by the edge of the stream. The house of Cioran's father, who was priest of Rashinari before he became protopope of Sibiu, is located at the edge of the water. It's yellow, with seven windows in the façade (two of them are strictly decorative), with two chimneys — it is largest and most imposing of the village. It can be recognized by the wrought iron cross that fills the space of one of the two false windows. Only one story, like all the other houses in town; the only two buildings having more than one floor are the school and the orthodox church, located side by side at the end of the street that starts at the priest's house and is called "Street of the protopope Emilian Cioran." More modestly, a plaque in honor of Emil, the writer, has just been posted in a corner of his first home, opposite a reproduction of Leonardo da Vinci's *Last Supper*, embedded in a black wall.

On his childhood in Rashinari, Cioran's friend the philosopher-Gabriel Liiceanu has written a useful little book, *Itinéraires d'une Vie: E.M. Cioran* (Michalon, 1995). "The Western bourgeois is an imbecile who thinks only of money," Emil wrote to his brother Aurel, 35 years after he moved to Paris. "Any of our shepherds is a greater philosopher than any intellectual from here." It should be said that one of Cioran's first contacts with Parisian intellectuals removed any illusion he might have had as to their mental capacities. In March 1947, he brought the manuscript of his first French text, the *Precis of Decomposition*, to a publisher. Albert Camus, whom he considered to be "if not a mediocre writer, then second-rate at best," read the manuscript and received the author, saying: "Now it's time for you to enter the circulation of ideas." And Cioran thought to himself, "Go to hell! He wanted to give me lessons, you understand, as if he were my teacher! He had read some writers, but he hadn't the least trace of philosophical culture," and he treated the young Romanian like "a poor neophyte come from the provinces."

Densus: St. Nicholas Church, Built in the XII Century

Răşinari: church

Cioran respected any work well done, and it was thus that he condemned the superficiality of Camus. A literary adviser at a big publishing house does not have the right to ignore the Masters of Thought.
The hierarchy of competences according to their degree of social re-
sponsibility: the antique honor of the artisans' guilds flared up one last
time in Cioran's indignation.

The manuscript sat in the Gallimard editorial offices for two
years; it was published only in 1949, because, meanwhile, its author had
received the Rivarol prize, an award given to the best French manuscript written by a foreigner.

The cemetery in Rashinari was one of young Emil's favorite places.
"The grave-digger was my friend. He was a very nice man and he knew
that my greatest pleasure was to receive craniums. When he was bury-

ing somebody, I would run immediately. . ." He would play football with death's-heads. Innocuous entertainment? Morbid kindness? Early obsession with death? As soon as you walk into the cemetery, on the left, one tomb stands on its own, imposing and very visible, containing the remains of the protopope, 1884-1957, and of his wife Elvira, 1888-1966. An inscription indicates that Aurel also plans to be buried here.

Cioran never went back to his village. After the years of high school in Sibiu, higher education in Bucharest and a year of teaching in Brashov, he left for Paris and never returned. He had just published a book, by which right-thinking people periodically seek to de-throne him; it was never translated into French, and for good reason. *The Transformation of Romania*, is a fascistic dream of national resurrection, later disavowed as an error of youth. Disgust with the weaknesses of the liberal State, hatred of parliamentarism, contempt for the conformity and passivity of the peasant, mystical worship of the "new man," all these ideas that swept the rest of Europe and caught up not a few intellectuals in the Messianic hope in "the leader," also agitated and tempted Cioran, who grew from this fleeting error to denounce all ideological creeds as impostures, whatever they may be, and professed a relentless skepticism.

The village spreads through the valley and climbs the lower slopes of a tall hill, Coasta Boacii, and the young Cioran used to enjoy walking to the top of the hill. It's a steep climb, between fir trees, to a meadow where some sheep are grazing. This is deep in the back-country, severe mountains covered with thick forests. Complete and proud isolation. Looking down at the village, you can confirm that there is not one ugly house in Rashinari, and the perfect harmony fills you with wonder.

But what good is this paradise, the teenager would ask, if the inhabits are constrained to live in medieval conditions? In 1995, the village was the same as it had been in 1920, as it had been a century or two before. The same crumbling streets, the same wooden carts, the same precariousness of existence. The priest's house, according to a man we met in the cemetery, was periodically flooded when the river rose. He told us that he had bought the house himself, but had to re-sell it because of the floods. Nothing has changed, nothing will ever change, be it kingdom, Soviet colony or democracy.

If we may ascribe to one's birthplace any influence on the formation of one's thought, I would suggest that the permanence, the time-lessness of Rashinari might have been the first model of what would become the *Precis of Decomposition, Syllogismes of Bitterness, The Temptation to Exist.* Closed in on itself, a savage negation of history, where all the illusions of progress are condemned without appeal: Cioran's work reflects his first experience of the world. Ripped out of his village and transplanted to the city, he never (he tells us) got over the shock. In this mourning I hear, more than the banal traumatism of being uprooted, the pain of knowing oneself to be forever interdependent with a useless perfection.

And certainly, if Cioran had been able to dine at Transylvania, the smart restaurant that was opened recently in Sibiu, the noisy good cheer of this establishment would have not changed one iota of his convictions.

Still talking about restaurants? A second Transylvania? One last time, yes, because the contrast between the majestic silence of Coasta Boacii and the sophisticated pretension of this room was so striking. It seems that it is in the restaurants that Romania is most frantically seeking to make up for lost time. You can identify the building by the line of taxis waiting outside — an odd sight in an otherwise quiet town. The dining room is vast, with the lights elegantly low. The cover charge is shocking, 15,000 lei per person. Excellent food, but service that is exasperatingly slow, apparently intentionally.

At 11:00 PM, there is a floor show. A curtain opens and a gent in a white suit comes out, with four dancing girls. The girls must be Lithuanians, says Norbert; this is a specialty of Lithuania. The performance isn't particularly vulgar, but it is a novelty in a location like this. What does it represent, to the handful of viewers at the tables next to us? Does it make them feel they are in tune with international modernity? Or, on the contrary, does it touch a vague nostalgia for the seraglios, the belly dances of the East?

1. See the biography of *La Princesse Bibesco*, by Ghislain de Diesbach, for an excellent evocation of Romania from before the war (Perrin, 1986).

2. Walter Starkie, *Les Racleurs du vent, avec les Tziganes de Puszta et de Transylvanie*, Phébus, 1995.

3. Claudio Magris, *The Danube*, L'Arpenteur, 1988.

OLTENIA

From Sibiu southward, in the direction of Craiova (the principal town of Oltenia), the road follows the course of the Olt, which has dug a narrow valley perpendicular to the southern Carpathans. Small monasteries, Byzantine in style, wedge themselves into the defile as best they can. The river runs past the foot of their walls. Glazed terracotta tiles decorate the outside of the church at Cornet. The monastery of Cozia, which is larger, has more refined decoration: carved window frames, rosettes, enamel ornaments inlaid in the mortar. The narthex rests upon five elegant arcades.

Leaving the Olt valley and making a sharp turn to the left, we set our course for Curtea de Argesh, a small city located at an altitude of 1250 feet, in the parallel valley of Argesh. Curtea de Argesh, capital of Wallachia until the end of the 14th century, contains two famous churches. The church of the princes, *Biserica Domneasca*, dates back to the first half of the 14th century. The floor plan is in the shape of a Greek cross, with a single cupola, and frescos; restoration work is underway. The caretaker, who talks nonstop, quotes Iorga and Mircea Eliade and tries to encourage us to stay longer in the damp chill of an empty nave; it pains him to see visitors preferring, to this modest building, the second church, known as the bishops', *Biserica episcopala*, which

Cozia: the church (F.F.)

is two centuries newer (dedicated in 1517) and was intended as a re-pository for the sovereigns' tombs.

Everything is odd here, and disconcerting. Instead of the tradi-tional floor plan of a Greek cross, there is a disproportionately large narthex, rectangular in form, which precedes the nave and a sanctuary in the shape of a trefoil. This narthex, which is wider than the nave, serves as the final resting place of Ferdinand I and his wife, the famous Queen Marie, of Carol I and Carmen Sylva, as well of older Wallachian princes. Two highly original turrets rise from the roof. The windows are high and narrow, and rather than standing vertically, they lean at oblique angles; the walls, carved with spiraling grooves with helical profiles, seem to be rotating giddily. The small cupola that tops these turrets seems to serve only one function — to keep them from capsiz-ing and falling over. 1517: an early taste for imbalance, for the precari-ous, a capricious freedom that would distinguish the baroque age.

The ornamentation of the façade is no less original. The gate and its frame resemble the entrance to a mosque. Blind arcades surround varicolored rosettes; gilded bronze doves holding little bells in their beaks — a symbol of the eucharist, the consecrated host. Two horizon-tal cornices go around the church. The upper one, decorated with sta-lactites, evokes the stucco filigree of the Arabs. The second one, made of a twisted roll, the *brâu,* girdles the church at middle height, would later become a characteristic element of late Romanian religious art. (We saw examples at Dragomirna, in Bukovina, Iashi, and Maramuresh.)

The whole thing is capped by two cupolas of a more traditional type, leaving an impression of absolute strangeness. It is simultane-ously solemn and fussy, a curious mixture of the Byzantine, the Muslim and the Indian! The oriental elements are undeniable. Louis Réau com-pares this church with St. Basil's Cathedral, with its bouquet of multi-colored domes on Red Square, in Moscow. But considering its cooler tone and the more sober colors, the square mass of the narthex, the whiteness of the marble, and the paved terrace that gives a base to the monument, I think of the Taj Mahal in Agra, which is similarly hieratic and mysterious.[*]

---

[*]The interior was ruined by Leconte de Nouÿ. The legends which surround the construc-tion of this church are discussed in Mircea Eliade's *Comments on the Legend of Master Manole* (Herne, 1994) and *De Zalmoxis with Gengis Khan* (Payot, 1970). Master Manole, the archi-tect, supposedly immured his wife, to prevent the church from collapsing: the mythical theme of the founder's sacrifice.

Curtea de Argeș: the cupolas of the XIV century church (F.F.)

From Curtea de Argesh we drive west toward Tirgu Jiu, stopping at several monasteries, of a type very different from the rest of Romania. They are more recent, built in the second half of the 17th century; they show the effects of contact with the West and a clear Italian influence. This is the style called Brancovan (named for Prince Constantin Brancoveanu, who built the castle at Mogoshoaia), and it is an amalgam (in religious as well as secular art) of the Byzantine and Renaissance styles.

Two stories of gantries surround the courtyard at the monastery of Horezu, which derives its name from the owls who live in the neighboring forests. The church, white and massive, is girdled around its middle by the *brâu*. At 4:30 PM, when we arrive, a nun in black is walking around the church striking the *toaca*. In a subtle and precise rhythm, she taps the board: three black, then a white note struck harder and higher up the board; then two black, short; a brief silence follows; after which the cadence of 3/1/2 begins again.

In the courtyard, novices are spreading out apples that they have picked in the orchard and cut in pieces for drying. Others are coming back from the edge of the fields with baskets of nuts. On the church façade are portraits of the project superintendents: architects, painters, etc.. This was an innovation. Inside, the Last Judgment presents realistic details previously unknown: teeth that clench, worms that torment the dead. Among the damned, in addition to the traditional heretics and infidels, we see a new category of rejects, those guilty of a moral failing, unworthy priests or dishonest merchants. Beautiful frescos in the refectory, too, which is dedicated to the Virgin. A devil shoots an arrow at a hermit, but an angel interposes its shield. A crowd of believers carrying their cross escorts Christ, others cast down their burdens and follow the Devil.

Night at *Dintr'un lemn*. This monastery is less prestigious, but it is charming, surrounded with roses. We are given a room with three beds, hung with fabrics in bright colors and furnished with a great ceramic heating stove in the corner, Russian-style, that will be lit while we eat in the refectory. The nuns, who do not eat with us, set the table with the products of the monastery. They serve us only what they have harvested from their fields, their orchard, their distillery. Their cattle shed has ten cows, a bull, and five calves. The menu is thus composed of an enormous dish of fried potatoes, some squares of *mamaliga*, a

Horezu: A Nun Sounding the Toaca (F.F.)

mountain of salted gherkins, all accompanied by a very strong plum brandy, the virulent *tsuica*. After these hospitable gestures, they have their evening mass. The sisters, most of them quite old, murmur their chants andprostrate themselves three or four times in a row, bowing to the ground with their creaking joints.

The following morning one of the mothers, Maica Paisia Iordacha, takes us into the tiny wooden church at the top of the garden. The monastery is named for this church, for it is made of the wood "of only one tree," *dintr'un lemn*. We decide to buy a copy of the pamphlet that reports this miracle, but the mother refuses to take our 200 *lei*, and asks us instead to send from France, in exchange for this memory, some paint brushes: she paints modern icons and cannot find the necessary materials here. Another mother, Maica Epitaria, ex-Superior, very authoritative, shows us the ring that she brought back from the gypsy festival, where she witnessed the crowning of the king. Our breakfast is another vegetarian farmland feast (boiled eggs, cheese, tomatoes, sweet peppers and warm milk). And then, we are back on the road.

In the Footsteps of Constantin Brancusi

Just as Bukovina has George Enescu, Moldova has Panaït Istrati, and Transylvania has Cioran, from Oltenia there emerged, in the person of Constantin Brancusi, the fourth great Romanian of modern times. A writer, a musician and a sculptor: the holy trilogy of creators and each one driven by a higher ambition than the desire to express his individuality. All three were of very humble origins; all three made it to Paris as soon as they could, while maintaining their spiritual demands and rejecting any compromise with the West. If Ionesco and Cioran represent the logical, analytical, occidental Romania, these other three drew their inspiration from the soil of the countryside and a mystical feeling for nature. With Enescu and Istrati, their Romanian roots are obvious, undeniable.

The work of Brancusi is more often misunderstood. It was said that, having discovered African art while in Paris, he started to draw the models for his statues in an extremely stylized way, with heads in the shape of shells. Louis Réau, usually an impeccable historian, dared to write (in 1946, still!) that "this quest for simplified volumes could be fertile if it were sincere; but one suspects in spite of oneself the secret desire to impress the bourgeois or to compete with the noisy fame of Picasso."

To make such an allegation, and to suspect of "Parisianism" someone who, throughout his exile remained a pure prophet, is to acknowledge knowing nothing of Romania, neither of the Romanian peasant culture, nor its ties with the East.

After a detour by Craiova, an unattractive industrial town whose museum does house some Brancusi sculptures including one version of the famous *Kiss*, we wanted to see where he had started out in life. Thus, before going to see the great monumental ensemble in Tirgu Jiu, the crowning glory of Brancusi's work, we set out for his native village. And that was well done, because once you have seen his town and his family home, you don't have to look any further to find "the sources" of his art; they are nowhere else but in this isolated hamlet of Oltenia.

Hobitsa, a couple of miles northwest of Tirgu Jiu, has just a few cottages. Constantin's grandfather built the church, off to the side, at the edge of the forest, in the cemetery where Grigori and Anna, the sculptor's brother and sister-in-law, are buried. In 1862, the father built by hand the house where Constantin was born fourteen years later. The house is made entirely of wood, including the shingled roof. A short gallery runs along the front. The father carved columns in it, and it is there that the child took the first model of what would be, some sixty years later, *The Endless Column* at Tirgu Jiu. Indeed, one may note, on the notched pillars, the decorative motif that inspired the son: the famous module made of two truncated pyramids joined at their bases. In Hobitsa, the format is more reduced, but the form is already perfect. One of the pillars is made of eleven modules, another of sixteen, another of eighteen. Each pillar finishes, at both ends, with a half module, as is the case at Tirgu Jiu.

The inside of the house consists of three rooms in a row: first a small storage room, then a big kitchen, and finally the living/sleeping room. This is the same layout as the Romanian churches': a narthex as entry, a nave where one meets, and a sanctuary, which is the private and place. This is an analogy that young Brancusi must have noticed, and must have helped imbue him with his interest in the mysteries of life and death and his desire to give a religious dimension to his creations. In the kitchen, the utensils evoke the rites of country life: a wolf

Brîncuşi's Table of Silence

trap, a cauldron for *mamaliga,* containers of *tsuica,* a salt box. Around the house, the traditional enclosure contains a corn shed, on pilings, and a distillery, both made of wood. On the monumental and ornately carved gate, some of the motifs are cut in modules identical to those on the pillars of the gallery.

Brancusi was born on February 17, 1876, during a snowstorm that buried Oltenia under a thick coat of silent whiteness. The excellent study by Radu Varia (*Brancusi,* Gallimard, 1989) recalls the early years of his education. He was into mischief and running away from the very start. From the age of eighteen to twenty-two, he attended the Trade

Brîncuşi's Gate of the Kiss

School in Craiova. He was initiated into freemasonry in 1894, more out
of a fascination with Egypt, with the East, one has to think, than with
any attraction for "rational doctrines." In 1898, he attended the Beaux
Arts school in Bucharest, while working as a dishwasher in a brasserie.
He spent some time in the dyeing workshops. In 1904, he set out, on
foot, for Paris. He fell ill, and wound up at a hospital in Lunéville; he
learned French from a book that was perfectly tailored to this pilgrim
of the absolute, *Isis Revealed*, by Helena Blavatsky. In Paris, his great
readings would include Vico, who gave him the theory of the never-
ending spiral and the eternal return, and *Jetsun-Kahbum*, an autobio-

graphical account by the Tibetan monk Jetsun Milarepa. He settled in Montparnasse, became friends with Ezra Pound, James Joyce, and the customs officer Rousseau. He spent three months in Rodin's studios, then rejected an art that he felt was too anthropocentrist. In spite of some "social lurches" (Radu Varia tells of a brief and stormy liaison with Marie Bonaparte, Princess George of Greece and a disciple of Freud), he always stayed true to his peasant values and spiritual inclination. Paul Morand, who is sometimes satisfied with superficial descriptions, got it right when he described the sculptor, after visiting his studio in 1926: he tells of "a long unkempt beard, which resembles that of Walt Whitman, eyes that combine a Latin cunning and Slavic mysticism, a gaze of kindness, certainty and courage, clothes that sat awkwardly on the body of a workman, of a logger, a stone mason," (*Papiers d'identité*, Grasset, 1931).

Brancusi dressed in blue, as a young man; later, he chose white. Every year, he celebrated his birthday with a meticulous three-day rite of purification: he would prepare a lustral bath, cut his hair and beard, dress in freshly laundered white underclothes and an overall as white as the snows of his native village. Before unveiling new works, he would conduct a ceremony of initiation. Summers, the nomad fled far from Paris, to the forests in central France. He would build a hut, or sometimes a rudimentary tree house, and live among the beasts and birds.

His first works were *The Prayer, The Wisdom of the Earth,* and *The Kiss.* From 1913 to 1922, he discovered and explored African art. Does that mean that Brancusi shared the trend that was popular among other artists working in Paris? Yes and no. To him, African art was a means of combating Western tradition, rejecting Greco-Roman humanism, and returning to the true nature of wood, renewing his ties with Romanian popular art. According to Radu Varia, the "demonic" aspect of Afican art repelled him, just as he considered Picasso "diabolic." In 1922, he removed all the works influenced by African art from his studio, gave up that route and returned to his true inspiration.

The forms that he invented, at the same time naked and incantatory, remain unique: ovoids *(The Sleeping Muse),* cubes *(The Kiss),* cylinders *(Torso of a Young Man),* fish or seals caught in their watery movement,

Brîncuşi's Endless Column

fluffy birds (another motif borrowed from Romanian carpets, our young friend Mihaï tells us — his nationalist sympathies would not brook any claim of African influence), roosters carved like light sensors. All reflect one goal: to deny matter, to capture space, to substitute for the anthropocentrism of traditional sculpture a cosmic possession of the infinite. Of his *Birds in Space*, reduced to a feather, to an aerodynamic flash, he said, "Like everything I have made, it struggles bitterly to rise up into the sky."

The high point in this rise is seen at Tirgu Jiu. We were anxious to discover what is not just a display of three monuments arranged in three points along a lengthy avenue, but an initiatory course, where each station must be appreciated, to be faithful to the thought of Brancusi. Alas, the ensemble was completely disfigured by the development policies of the communist authorities. After stopping at *The Table of Silence*, we should have walked to *The Gate of the Kiss*, before hiking further toward *The Endless Column*. But that is impossible today: a housing development has been built between the gate and the column; from the latter, isolated on a concrete traffic circle, first two monuments could not even be seen; and, to go from the gate to the column, we had to get back in the car and drive around what has become part of the city, and find our way between dreadful buildings. Never has the massacre of a work of genius been more consciously perpetrated. France itself lent a hand to this crime, since *The Blue Guide* of 1966 (which takes a very favorable line with regard to Ceausescu — this was the era when Nixon and de Gaulle were taking care of Ceausescu), which was not printed after 1989, provides these lines of misinformation: "The city preserves some monumental works of the great sculptor, . . . At the entrance to the city park, the arch of *The Kiss* rises. . . . In the axis of the monument, a long alley opens. . . which ends at *The Table of Silence*." Following paragraph: "East of the city, in a garden, Brancusi's *The Endless Column* rises, 90 feet high."

No, no and no! This is not a question of "some" monuments, but of a coherent ensemble, a homogeneous whole, imagined and realized in one flash of brilliance, from one spiritual unity. The course does not start at the *Arch* (or *Gate*) *of the Kiss*, but at *The Table of Silence*, and the column, the goal and the apotheosis of the trajectory, is not located "East of the city," but in the extension of the ransacked triumphal avenue, at the end of the road that leaves the table and passes under the gate.

Brancusi had calculated everything, according to the law of the golden mean, with the meticulousness of a geometrician and the obsession of a mystic. The total length of the course: 1,653 meters. The distance between the table and the gate: 160 meters. Between the gate and the column: 1,493 meters.

The Table of Silence is designed as two superimposed circular slabs: 215 cm diameter for the higher flagstone, 200 for the lower flagstone. The first is 45 cm thick, the second is 40. The twelve stone seats that surround the table, made of two halves of a sphere joined at the middle of their convex sides, are 45 cm in diameter. They are 120 cm away from the table, and 120 cm away from each other. Does the table look like the sun, from which emanate the twelve vital rays to illuminate the world? Do the twelve knights of the Round Table come here to swear their oaths anew? The twelve Apostles sup, to seal again their alliance? Maybe we don't need to look that hard for a symbolic significance. I remember seeing, in the enclosure of the church of Patrauti in Bukovina, a comparable assembly of stones. A half-sphere is positioned in the grass, flat side down, topped with a circular slab. Around this table, there are seven round stones as seats. The ensemble dates from the 15th century, and could be one "source" of *The Table of Silence*; or it could be sheer coincidence, both works equally derived from the funds of Romanian mythology.

The Gate of the Kiss is made up of three massive stone parallelepipeds (a six-sided form in which each facet is a parallelogram), engraved with hieroglyphics; it is designed according to calculations that are no less precise, starting from a 85 cm module: 170 cm for the height of the lintel, and each pillar measuring 340 cm tall and 170 cm wide. According to Radu Varia, the allusion to Egyptian temples is manifest: the kiss, illustrated by the arc, signifies the passage from one spirit to another spirit, the exchange between two souls, the sublimation of the erotic instinct in spiritual exaltation. The hieroglyphics on the lintel reproduce forty times the Brancusian motif of the *Kiss*, stylized here as laconically as the signs engraved on the walls of Dendur or Abdu.

Lastly, the column. It's almost thirty meters high and includes sixteen modules, fifteen of them built by joining two truncated pyramids by their bases. The measuring unit is the same as for the table and the seats of the first station, 45 cm. Thus the truncated part of the pyramid is 45 cm, and twice 45 cm for the base, with four times 45 cm for the total height of the module. The column ends at top and bottom with a half-module, like the rustic pillars of Hobitsa. The material is bronze-plated cast iron, over an armature of steel. "What was your purpose in erecting the *Endless Column?*" someone asked Brancusi. "To support the vault of heaven." He was not mad; he was simply expressing the humor and the wisdom of his native land. He was truly delighted when an admirer exclaimed, about the ovoid in front of her, all polish and sheen: "It is even more beautiful than a fireman's helmet." The mixture of rural materialism (he considered himself an artisan more than an artist), of popular cunning and an aspiration toward the cosmos is what makes Brancusi so attractive. Now that his studio in Beaubourg has finally been re-opened, the contradictory and complementary aspects of his personality are more easily appreciated than in the usual museum displays, since the work itself is essentially rebellious and defies museological classification.

Without end, this column, because it represents a cosmic lift-off, the liberation of the heart, after preparation through meditation (the round table) and intensified by love (the gate), the deliverance from any carnal bond; propulsion into the infinite.

The stone mason who helped Brancusi in his work at Tirgu Jiu reported that the sculptor kept a stockpile of apples in his room, and every morning he would stuff his pockets with them. Then at the stroke of noon, he would sit down in the middle of the construction site and bite into them, ceremoniously enjoying the crunch. The last project, which he did not have time to realize, was to build a mausoleum in the shape of an apple for the Maharajah of Indore. The same "desire for India" that Panaït Istrati refers to in *The Pilgrim of the Heart*, and Mircea Eliade in *Promises of the Equinox.*

Apple, sphere, module, upward rhythm, vital breath: images of immortality. In Tirgu Jiu, two Romanias clash: the mystical Romania, orientalized, which brought something new to Europe, and the industrialized Romania, utilitarian, limited, and vandal, which used its power to ruin the sublime Utopia of the greatest Romanian artist. Around *The Table of Silence,* this second Romania has installed woodplank flooring, transforming a place of meditation into a picnic spot; through *The Gate of the Kiss,* it's not the sky that one sees now, but cars and concrete; *The Endless Column,* on a backdrop of urban construction, is nothing but an absurd signpost.

But the apple remains. Apples. Apples, that children offered to us, in front of their houses, throughout our trips. Apples, that the women retired in convents dry for winter. Apples, that never ran short even during the most severe shortages. Apples, that summarize so well the compact, smooth, rural and solid universe of Brancusi and symbol-ize at the same time his dream of modular perfection. Like everything that we found so appealing in Romania, the apple speaks to the senses, but above all to the soul.

Acknowledgements

The authors and the editor wish to express their gratitude to the following people, who assisted this project in so many ways:

Carmen Firan (New York)
Svetlana Ciuca
Georges Diener
Didier Dutour
Radu Ionescu
Paul Laffon
Frederic Martel
Ion Munteanu
Alex Leo Serban
Dolores and Radu Toma
Renaud Vignal

Ieud: the church

Also from Algora Publishing:

CLAUDIU A. SECARA
THE NEW COMMONWEALTH
From Bureaucratic Corporatism to Socialist Capitalism

The notion of an elite-driven worldwide perestroika has gained some credibility lately. The book examines in a historical perspective the most intriguing dialectic in the Soviet Union's "collapse" — from socialism to capitalism and back to socialist capitalism — and speculates on the global implications.

IGNACIO RAMONET
THE GEOPOLITICS OF CHAOS

The author, Director of *Le Monde Diplomatique,* presents an original, discriminating and lucid political matrix for understanding what he calls the "current disorder of the world" in terms of Internationalization, Cyberculture and Political Chaos.

TZVETAN TODOROV
A PASSION FOR DEMOCRACY –
Benjamin Constant

The French Revolution rang the death knell not only for a form of society, but also for a way of feeling and of living; and it is still not clear as yet what did we gain from the changes.

MICHEL PINÇON & MONIQUE PINÇON-CHARLOT
GRAND FORTUNES –
Dynasties of Wealth in France

Going back for generations, the fortunes of great families consist of far more than money— they are also symbols of culture and social interaction. In a nation known for democracy and meritocracy, piercing the secrets of the grand fortunes verges on a crime of lèse-majesté . . . *Grand Fortunes* succeeds at that.

CLAUDIU A. SECARA
TIME & EGO –
Judeo-Christian Egotheism and the Anglo-Saxon Industrial Revolution

The first question of abstract reflection that arouses controversy is the problem of Becoming. Being persists, beings constantly change; they are born and they pass away. How can Being change and yet be eternal? The quest for the logical and experimental answer has just taken off.

JEAN-MARIE ABGRALL
SOUL SNATCHERS: The Mechanics of Cults

Jean-Marie Abgrall, a psychiatrist and a criminologist, is Europe's foremost expert on cults. He serves as an expert witness to the French Court of Appeals, and is frequently consulted by the European judicial and legislative authorities. The fruit of fifteen years of research, his book delivers the first methodical analysis of the cult phenomenon, decoding the mental manipulation on behalf of mystified observers as well as victims.

JEAN-CLAUDE GUILLEBAUD
THE TYRANNY OF PLEASURE

Guillebaud, a Sixties' radical, re-thinks liberation, taking a hard look at the question of sexual morals -- that is, the place of the forbidden -- in a modern society. For almost a whole generation, we have lived in the illusion that this question had ceased to exist. Today the illusion is faded, but a strange and tumultuous distress replaces it. No longer knowing very clearly where we stand, our societies painfully seek answers between unacceptable alternatives: bold-faced permissiveness or nostalgic moralism.

SOPHIE COIGNARD AND MARIE-THÉRÈSE GUICHARD
FRENCH CONNECTIONS –
The Secret History of Networks of Influence

They were born in the same region, went to the same schools, fought the same fights and made the same mistakes in youth. They share the same morals, the same fantasies of success and the same taste for money. They act behind the scenes to help each other, boosting careers, monopolizing business and information, making money, conspiring and, why not, becoming Presidents!

VLADIMIR PLOUGIN
RUSSIAN INTELLIGENCE SERVICES. Vol. I. Early Years

This collection contains the latest works by historians, investigating the most mysterious episodes from Russia's past. All essays are based on thorough studies of preserved documents. The book discusses the establishment of secret services in Kievan Rus, and describes heroes and systems of intelligence and counterintelligence in the 16th-17th centuries. Semen Maltsev, a diplomat of Ivan the Terrible's times is presented as well as the story of the abduction of "Princess Tarakanova".

JEAN-JACQUES ROSA
EURO ERROR

The European Superstate makes Jean-Jacques Rosa mad, for two reasons. First, actions taken to relieve unemployment have created inflation, but have not reduced unemployment. His second argument is even more intriguing: the 21st century will see the fragmentation of the U. S., not the unification of Europe.

ANDRÉ GAURON
EUROPEAN MISUNDERSTANDING

Few of the books decrying the European Monetary Union raise the level of the discussion to a higher plane. *European Misunderstanding* is one of these. Gauron gets it right, observing that the real problem facing Europe is its political future, not its economic future.

EDITOR: BERNARD-HENRI LÉVY
WHAT GOOD ARE INTELLECTUALS?
44 Writers Share Their Thoughts

An intimate dialogue with some of the world's best minds, in the form of essays, interviews and responses to the oft-asked question, "What good are intellectuals?" 44 of the world's most respected authors reflect on life, death and meaning. Authors include: Nadine Gordimer, Ivan Klima, Arthur Miller, Czeslaw Milosz, Joyce Carol Oates, Cynthia Ozick, Octavio Paz, Salman Rushdie, Susan Sontag, William Styron, Mario Vargas Llosa, and others.

DOMINIQUE FERNANDEZ
PHOTOGRAPHER: FERRANTE FERRANTI
ROMANIAN RHAPSODY — *An Overlooked Corner of Europe*

"Romania doesn't get very good press." And so, renowned French travel writer Dominique Fernandez and top photographer Ferrante Ferranti head out to form their own images. In four long journeys over a 6-year span, they uncover a tantalizing blend of German efficiency and Latin nonchalance, French literature and Gypsy music, Western rationalism and Oriental mysteries. Fernandez reveals the rich Romanian essence. Attentive and precise, he digs beneath the somber heritage of communism to reach the deep roots of a European country that is so little-known.

PHILIPPE TRÉTIACK
ARE YOU AGITÉ? *Treatise on Everyday Agitation*

"A book filled with the exuberance of a new millennium, full of humor and relevance. Philippe Trétiack, a leading reporter for *Elle*, goes around the world and back, taking an interest in the futile as well as the essential. His flair for words, his undeniable culture, help us to catch on the fly what we really are: characters subject to the ballistic impulse of desires, fads and a click of the remote. His book invites us to take a healthy break from the breathless agitation in general." —*Aujourd'hui le Parisien*

"The 'Agité,' that human species that lives in international airports, jumps into taxis while dialing the cell phone, eats while clearing the table, reads the paper while watching TV and works during vacation – has just been given a new title." —*Le Monde des Livres*

PAUL LOMBARD
VICE & VIRTUE — *Men of History, Great Crooks for the Greater Good*

Personal passion has often guided powerful people more than the public interest. With what result? From the courtiers of Versailles to the back halls of Mitterand's government, from Danton — revealed to have been a paid agent for England — to the shady bankers of Mitterand's era, from the buddies of Mazarin to the builders of the Panama Canal, Paul Lombard unearths the secrets of the corridors of power. He reveals the vanity and the corruption, but also the grandeur and panache that characterize the great. This cavalcade over many centuries can be read as a subversive tract on how to lead.

RICHARD LABÉVIÈRE
DOLLARS FOR TERROR — *The U.S. and Islam*

"In this riveting, often shocking analysis, the U.S. is an accessory in the rise of Islam, because it manipulates and aids radical Moslem groups in its shortsighted pursuit of its economic interests, especially the energy resources of the Middle East and the oil- and mineral-rich former Soviet republics of Central Asia. Labévière shows how radical Islamic fundamentalism spreads its influence on two levels, above board, through investment firms, banks and shell companies, and clandestinely, though a network of drug dealing, weapons smuggling and money laundering. This important book sounds a wake-up call to U.S. policy-makers." —*Publishers Weekly*

JEANNINE VERDÈS-LEROUX
DECONSTRUCTING PIERRE BOURDIEU
Against Sociological Terrorism From the Left

Sociologist Pierre Bourdieu went from widely-criticized to widely-acclaimed, without adjusting his hastily constructed theories. Turning the guns of critical analysis on his own critics, he was happier jousting in the ring of (often quite undemocratic) political debate than reflecting and expanding upon his own propositions. Verdès-Leroux has spent 20 years researching the policy impact of intellectuals who play at the fringes of politics. She suggests that Bourdieu arrogated for himself the role of "total intellectual" and proved that a good offense is the best defense. A pessimistic Leninist bolstered by a ponderous scientific construct, Bourdieu stands out as the ultimate doctrinaire more concerned with self-promotion than with democratic intellectual engagements.

HENRI TROYAT
TERRIBLE TZARINAS

Who should succeed Peter the Great? Upon the death of this visionary and despotic reformer, the great families plotted to come up with a successor who would surpass everyone else — or at least, offend none. But there were only women — Catherine I, Anna Ivanovna, Anna Leopoldovna, Elizabeth I. These autocrats imposed their violent and dissolute natures upon the empire, along with their loves, their feuds, their cruelties. Born in 1911 in Moscow, Troyat is a member of the Académie française, recipient of Prix Goncourt.

JEAN-MARIE ABGRALL
HEALERS OR STEALERS — Medical Charlatans

Jean-Marie Abgrall is Europe's foremost expert on cults and forensic medicine. He asks, are fear of illness and death the only reasons why people trust their fates to the wizards of the pseudo-revolutionary and the practitioners of pseudo-magic? We live in a bazaar of the bizarre, where everyday denial of rationality has turned many patients into ecstatic fools. While not all systems of nontraditional medicine are linked to cults, this is one of the surest avenues of recruitment, and the crisis of the modern world may be leading to a new mystique of medicine where patients check their powers of judgment at the door.

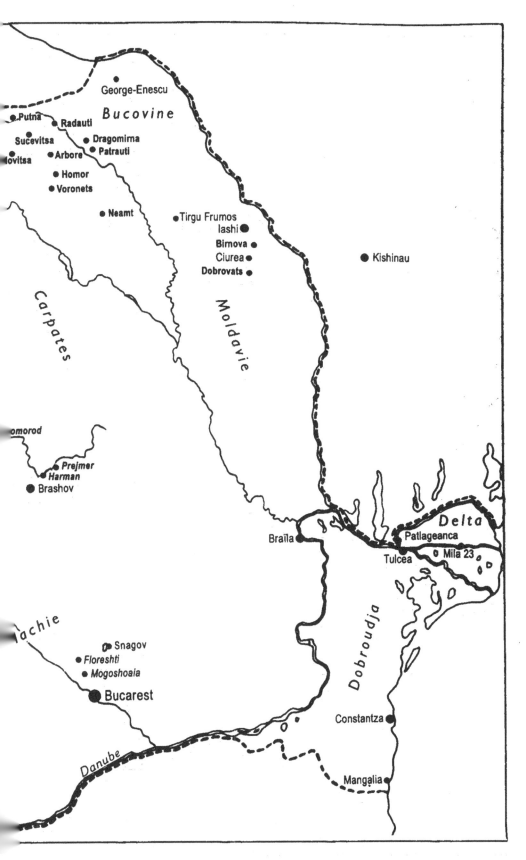

Printed in the United States
by Baker & Taylor Publisher Services